Moving Toward the Future of Policing

Gregory F. Treverton, Matt Wollman, Elizabeth Wilke, Deborah Lai

RAND NATIONAL SECURITY RESEARCH DIVISION

The research described in this report was conducted within the RAND Center for Global Risk and Security under the auspices of the International Programs of the RAND Corporation.

Library of Congress Control Number: 2011939018.

ISBN: 978-0-8330-5320-6

The RAND Corporation is a nonprofit institution that helps improve policy and decisionmaking through research and analysis. RAND's publications do not necessarily reflect the opinions of its research clients and sponsors.

RAND® is a registered trademark.

© Copyright 2011 RAND Corporation

Permission is given to duplicate this document for personal use only, as long as it is unaltered and complete. Copies may not be duplicated for commercial purposes. Unauthorized posting of RAND documents to a non-RAND website is prohibited. RAND documents are protected under copyright law. For information on reprint and linking permissions, please visit the RAND permissions page (http://www.rand.org/publications/permissions.html).

Published 2011 by the RAND Corporation
1776 Main Street, P.O. Box 2138, Santa Monica, CA 90407-2138
1200 South Hayes Street, Arlington, VA 22202-5050
4570 Fifth Avenue, Suite 600, Pittsburgh, PA 15213-2665
RAND URL: http://www.rand.org/
To order RAND documents or to obtain additional information, contact
Distribution Services: Telephone: (310) 451-7002;
Fax: (310) 451-6915; Email: order@rand.org

Preface

This book grew out of conversations with members of the Advisory Board of RAND's Center for Global Risk and Security. It began when one board member who is now a co-author of this book, Matt Wollman, observed that when asked what their police forces will look like in 20 years, police chiefs almost always say "much like now," perhaps with some adjustments in balances of gender and ethnicity. It seemed to us that this couldn't be the right answer, given advances in technology, especially, but also in operating concepts by police authorities. Thus was born this book, an effort to think creatively but also usefully about the future. It draws on the work of many others to create a vision of what future policing could look like, but it also concludes with concrete steps for moving toward that vision. It is aimed at those who make decisions in shaping law enforcement organizations, their equipment, training, and concepts of operations, as well as at potential partners in the private sector. It should also be of interest to concerned citizens, whose support is absolutely essential to effective policing. This book results from the generosity of donors to the center. We greatly appreciate their support, and we also thank Queenisha Rynders for her research assistance early in the project.

This research was conducted within the RAND Center for Global Risk and Security, part of International Programs at the RAND Corporation. The center aims to improve public policy by providing decisionmakers and the public with rigorous, objective research on critical, crosscutting policy issues affecting global risk and security.

For more information on the RAND Center for Global Risk and Security, see http://www.rand.org/international_programs/cgrs.html or contact the director (contact information is provided on the web page).

Contents

Figures

Tables

Summary

Imagine a future investigation of a home invasion robbery. En route to responding to the call, the police officer—she might now be called a customer service representative—searches databases and, while she drives, hears descriptions of any recent relevant incidents in the neighborhood, calls from the house, and previous law enforcement visits. The victims are not hurt, and they provide some description of the perpetrators and their methods. One of the victims also managed to get a slightly dark cell phone picture of one of the thieves in profile. The officer arrives and images the scene for fingerprints. She enters all this information and the cell phone photo in her smartphone, and, by the time she gets back to her car, her report has been filed. Descriptions, methods, prints, and picture are all being matched against information in existing databases. By the time she is moving, a match has been found, the suspect's last address has been identified, and a search has begun based on his cell phone number and location.

Vision of the Future

This vision of the future of policing is not all that futuristic. Most of the technologies are with us today, or soon will be. Some dimensions of this future—for instance, geographical police jurisdictions that less and less precisely match crime's reach across boundaries—have long been with us and will continue to be with us, but they are not immutable. A third dimension that will frame the future is also here: Criminals and criminal organizations are adaptive. They will continue to look for seams in public safety defenses, and they will become more and more networked, thus able to learn what works more quickly. They will adapt even if we do not. The three dimensions together—jurisdiction, technology, and threat—suggest very different concepts of police operations, some of which also are here, in part, today.

Policing has transformed in the past and so can do it again. Its history can be divided into four overlapping eras. In the political era (most of the nineteenth century), policing was guided by law, but close and mutually beneficial ties between the policing force and politicians resulted in high levels of corruption—hardly surprisingly. As a reaction, in the reform era, which began early in the twentieth century, policing emulated J. Edgar Hoover's restructuring of the Federal Bureau of Investigation (FBI), aiming to become less political, more professional, and narrower in scope; as a result, police became less involved in providing social services to the communities they served. The reform era also saw the beginning of serious efforts to collect and study data on crime.

However, the spike in the nation's crime rate that began in the 1960s undermined confidence in the measures of the reform era. Research suggested that neither preventive patrol nor rapid response was effective. At the same time, issues of racial and gender discrimination boiled up on the political agenda, and these issues further increased the disillusionment with the so-called "objective" policing practices of the reform era, at least for many of America's citizens. For instance, a 1968 *Detroit Free Press* survey revealed that police brutality was the number one problem that blacks felt they faced in the months leading up to the July 1967 riots.

The result was yet another transition in policing, to an era of community-based or problem-solving policing that reemphasized good relations with the local community. Perhaps the most debated approach of this era was order-maintenance policing (OMP). In "Broken Windows" in 1982, George Kelling and James Q. Wilson posited that "fixing broken windows," or preventing public disorder, would not only establish a norm against crime in a neighborhood but also convey to the public that the police was invested in the community. OMP led to a variety of policing initiatives in the 1990s. In 1994,

New York City instituted CompStat, an initiative to hold local commanders accountable for achieving crime reduction goals in their areas, which Police Commissioner William Bratton and others credited for the decrease in crime in the city. The problem-oriented component of this era emphasized analysis as a crucial ingredient in framing effective policing strategies.

The fourth era, intelligence-led policing (ILP), traces its lineage back to Britain in the 1980s but was reinvigorated by the emergence of terrorism as a threat. That threat adds a new mission to policing, but in other respects ILP has much in common with community-based policing: Both require the support of the community; both require better communication and information-sharing within and across public safety institutions; and both seek to improve policing through analysis of empirical evidence, facilitated by better and faster technologies—the movement toward evidence-based policing and the quest for "predictive policing." The terrorist threat is at the margins of this book, but, in driving ILP, it does reinforce the vision of policing set out in this book.

More-dramatic parts of that vision are also already with us, at least in part. ILP suggests a form of deterrence based less on the presence of police on the beat than on an increased risk for criminals of being caught. It also indicates a changed balance between policing's front office—the customer service representative described earlier—and its back office, especially analysts and those who manage databases. Outsourcing of some police functions is on the rise, and it suggests a changed balance between sworn officers and civilians. It also hints at new possibilities for partnership.

Companies are now developing niche capacities for policing: Palantir, for instance, is a company built by creators of PayPal that specializes in "smart searches" of large amounts of data while meeting the privacy and civil liberties standards of federal law; another company, 3VR, aims to become the "Google of surveillance video" by creating "pictures" that are a fully searchable virtual template of facial features. But imagine if Google or another technology giant wanted to become policing's valued partner across a wide range of functions and departments. The economies of scale would dwarf those now present when departments share outsourcing for a single function, such as finance.

Privacy concerns would also loom large. Could they be managed, along with lines of accountability?

Drivers of the Vision: Jurisdiction, Technology, and Threat

Policing is mismatched to crime, for it is still primarily organized by geography, while crime is not. At one extreme, the bank robbed in a cyber crime may be in New York, but the criminals may be in Estonia, operating through a half dozen computers that they have commandeered in six different parts of the globe. At the other, Santa Monica is surrounded by Los Angeles but has its own police force. Most sharing of information is driven by particular crimes; routine sharing is rare. As late as 2009, Santa Monica also had different communications networks than Culver City, five miles away, and so found communication difficult. If working across borders in a single metropolitan region is hard, imagine working across international borders. The U.S.-Mexico border is a stark example, for it becomes as much a seam in police defenses and a sanctuary for criminals as it is a protection.

Two features of technology and policing are striking. The first is that, until recently, the innovations that changed policing the most—from automobiles to telephones to computers—were not invented for police or to improve policing. Rather, they were invented to make everyday life easier or richer. The second is that whatever technologies the police employ, the criminals can too. The key to the future of policing, then, is not technology but the ways in which police forces adapt it to their purposes. At its core, technology has the potential to change (1) data and intelligence gathering, (2) problem-solving processes, (3) partnership structures, and (4) departmental organization.

The globalization of commerce and technology has helped to fundamentally alter the nature of the threat to society from crime. The threat will continue to morph. Criminals are now able to commit crimes, such as identity theft, from home that previously required teams of people and intense coordination. Individuals and small groups can commit major crimes and thus are changing what "organized crime" means. Technology-enabled crime has arrived and will continue to develop. And the next step, "virtual" crimes, is not far off; already there are harbingers of that new arena of crime. At the same time, "old" crimes are evolving as to be almost completely distinct from the real-world crimes from which they emerged. For example, what amounts to bank robbery can be done virtually, with no need for guns, money bags, and escape cars. In addition, the environment in which criminals operate will morph as technology, law, and law enforcement change. None of these dimensions operates independently of the others; they are all interconnected in complex ways.

Moving Toward the Vision

The following are concrete steps that police departments and other public safety agencies can take to move toward the vision, along with examples, both suggestive and cautionary:

Educate personnel and leaders. Building internal support for change is critical. For instance, police organizations thought preventive patrol was effective until analysis of data revealed very little difference among patrol patterns. Just as officers are taught how to spot an intoxicated driver, they should learn how to use technology: In some cities all patrol cars are equipped with fingerprint kits, and police are taught how to use the Automated Finger Print Identification System, a computerized system for matching fingerprint specimens. Education will be especially important as human resource needs change. Departments will need more data scientists to deal with large amounts of personal data and more security clearances to deal with sensitive information.

The use and exchange of possible sensitive personal data on suspects, criminals, and civilians will entail a strong commitment to data safety. The increasing interconnectedness of departments brings many benefits but also creates more vulnerabilities by which data can become insecure. It also obscures lines of responsibility for data and information. Data management plans will need to be constructed and implemented to ensure that the information that is being transferred across partnership networks is not compromised.

Police leaders will have to change culturally to accept integration as well. Police personnel will have to learn alternative ways of interacting with the public effectively—for instance, the Boston Police Department and its Twitter feed. With increased community involvement will come increased volume of communication and interaction between police personnel and citizens. This means that the majority of police personnel—not just officers working the street beats—will need training in customer service and client interaction in order to effectively engage the community.

Transition to common technical platforms. This should be low-hanging fruit but does not always seem to be. According to one assessment, the gaps across jurisdictions, like those detailed in Los Angeles, can now be overcome, and connecting the department with every other law enforcement agency operating in or around the jurisdiction should be the goal. While ILP, in general, requires integration of information from many intelligence-gathering entities, integration does not necessarily require a common technical platform. It does require at least a common platform for sharing information. Interpol and other cooperative initiatives can facilitate this process, and bilateral working arrangements are on the rise—for instance, allowing officers from other jurisdictions to pursue investigations across those jurisdictions even when the jurisdiction lines are national borders.

In Los Angeles, the LA-SafetyNet initiative aimed to connect 34,000 first responders across the county's different police, fire, and public health jurisdictions. Yet these initial efforts are being constructed before there is any broad agreement on standards for equipment and networks. As a result, there is no guarantee that other jurisdictions that seek to join the networks in the future will be operating, literally, on the same wavelength. Los Angeles County pioneered these efforts with the Terrorism Early Warning group, which began in the mid-1990s. It was explicitly designed to anticipate emerging threats, especially terrorism, and to try to deny networked adversaries the advantage of working in the seams of existing policing organizations. It sought to blend networking with traditional organization by including law enforcement, fire service, and health authorities at all levels of government.

Biometrics, like blood samples, iris scans, and DNA typing, may come to replace fingerprinting as cheaper, more-precise ways of identifying criminals. They may also be able to serve as unique identifiers across databases, yielding more-accurate cross-database search results. The advent and rapid improvement of database management and biometric technology facilitates information exchange. The FBI is in the process of developing a database of biometrics called Next Generation Identification that will share standards held by Britain, Canada, Australia, and New Zealand and will interface with the National Crime Information Center database to further the goal of instant and seamless cross-border information-sharing.

Leverage winning technologies. Over time, these winning technologies are those used for collecting, sorting, storing, and recalling information. Computer terminals in their cars, followed by handheld devices, have given officers on patrol access to information systems, enabling them to check quickly for stolen vehicles or outstanding warrants. Smartphones and mobile computing systems are likely to have a major impact, as are improvements in camera technology and programs designed to interface with them. Supercomputing—the ability to store, categorize, and retrieve massive amounts of data in a few seconds—will be the next step in transforming police investigations. The searchable data stored by programs like 3VR's could save hundreds of man-hours and free up human resources for tasks that computers cannot do. Not only can cameras hooked up to powerful software detect facial and other identifying features, but they can also be programmed to "learn" normal human behavior in order to detect unusual or suspicious behavior.

Leverage changing interactions and relations between police, the public, and the private sector. For example, to address its shortcomings in video surveillance, the Dallas Police Department Narcotics Unit turned to the private sector; a detective from the Technical Operations Unit worked with a local company to devise a new and improved video system. AT&T partnered with the FBI to allow it access to AT&T's call records after 9/11. When Mississippi Senator John Burton's Chevy Impala was stolen, he called OnStar. OnStar then called the police. When officers had the vehicle in sight, they requested that Stolen Vehicle Slowdown be initiated, and the vehicle was safely slowed to a stop. Several technology firms and financial companies have regular meetings with police officials in the areas in which they operate in order to keep police abreast of new and emerging trends—for example, in identity fraud. The Boston Police Department has a weblog and a Twitter feed to alert Bostonians to activities of interest and keep them informed of goings-on in the city.

Draw maximum benefit from federal leadership and funding. Here, the spillover from the fight against terror is positive, providing both funding and some leadership. To be sure, terrorism gets a much larger share of resources than its societal damage would warrant, but departments have turned that aid into all-hazards assistance. Terrorism also spurs the trend toward intelligence-based policing. It also provides incentive for integrated efforts. The story of the public safety wireless network is still unfinished, but the transition from analog to digital television at least freed up space on the spectrum for an integrated public safety network. For all their shortcomings, the fusion centers are another example. They are intended to complement the joint terrorism task forces (JTTFs). JTTFs work on cases once they are identified, and the fusion centers are meant to assemble strategic intelligence at the regional level and pass the appropriate information on to the investigators in the task forces.

Acknowledgments

We thank the many police officials with whom we were in touch during the course of this project. We especially appreciate the work of our reviewers, Lt. John Sullivan of the Los Angeles Sheriff's Department and our RAND colleague Gregory Ridgeway. They did us the great service of not only correcting errors but also directing us to additional materials and anecdotes to drive home our central themes. Of course, any remaining shortcomings are ours alone.

Abbreviations

ACLU	American Civil Liberties Union
CCTV	closed-circuit television
CIA	Central Intelligence Agency
CompStat	computer statistics
ConOps	concepts of operations
CPD	Cincinnati Police Department
DDoS	distributed denial of service
DEA	Drug Enforcement Administration
DHS	Department of Homeland Security
EU	European Union
FBI	Federal Bureau of Investigation
FCC	Federal Communications Commission
FIG	Field Intelligence Group
FINCEN	Financial Crimes Enforcement Network
FIU	financial intelligence unit
GPS	Global Positioning System
I&W	Indications and Warning

IACP	International Association of Chiefs of Police
ILP	intelligence-led policing
IT	information technology
JRIC	Joint Regional Intelligence Center
JTTF	Joint Terrorism Task Force
LAPD	Los Angeles Police Department
LASD	Los Angeles County Sheriff's Department
MHz	megahertz
MMOG	massive multiplayer online game
NCIC	National Crime Information Center
NCIS	National Criminal Intelligence Service
NGA	National Geospatial-Intelligence Agency
NSA	National Security Agency
NSB	National Security Branch
NYPD	New York Police Department
OMP	order-maintenance policing
PCTF	Police Chiefs' Task Force
PDA	personal digital assistant
POP	problem-oriented policing
SCI	Secret Compartmented Intelligence
TARA	Trans America Ventures Associates
TEC	technology-enabled crime
TEW group	Terrorism Early Warning group
TTPs	tactics, techniques, and procedures

UAV	unmanned aerial vehicle
VCF	Virtual Case File
WoW	World of Warcraft

CHAPTER ONE

Framing the Future

Imagine a future investigation of a home invasion robbery. En route to responding to the call, the police officer—she might now be called a customer service representative—searches databases and, while she drives, hears descriptions of any recent relevant incidents in the neighborhood, calls from the house, and previous law enforcement visits. The victims are not hurt, and they provide some description of the perpetrators and their methods. One of the victims also managed to get a slightly dark cell phone picture of one of the thieves in profile. The officer arrives and images the scene for fingerprints. She enters all this information and the cell phone photo in her smartphone, and, by the time she gets back to her car, her report has been filed. Descriptions, methods, prints, and picture are all being matched against information in existing databases. By the time she is moving, a match has been found, the suspect's last address has been identified, and a search has begun based on his cell phone number and location.

Now, let us return to the present. On September 30, 2010, David Hartley and his wife were jet-skiing at Falcon Lake, which straddles the U.S.-Mexico border in Texas. They were photographing a semisubmerged old church on the Mexican side of the lake when armed men in two or three boats approached. The Hartleys attempted to flee, but the men opened fire, hitting David twice in the head. His wife said she wanted to recover his body but had to race for her own life. His body was not found. The mystery only deepened when the decapitated head of the Tamaulipas state investigator on the case was delivered in a suitcase to the Mexican military's headquarters in Reynosa on October 12 (Stewart, 2010).

From the start, there were suspicions that drug traffickers were involved. The area of the lake in which the Hartleys were attacked had also been the site of fighting between the Gulf Cartel and their onetime enforcers, Los Zetas—a collection of renegade former police, Central American special forces veterans, and gang members; brutal killers, but ones armed with satellite trackers, antiaircraft weapons, and the ability to monitor the conversations of local politicians. David Hartley's death may never be solved, but it could have been a case of mistaken identity. The Hartleys had hauled their jet skis to the lake in a truck with license plates from Tamaulipas, and the couple may have been taken by a low-level Zeta as a Gulf Cartel reconnaissance team. The beheading of the investigator was a warning to Mexican authorities not to investigate while Los Zetas conducted their own damage-control operation.

Both of these are possible visions of future police operations. The point to take from these examples is that if police organizations do not adapt, the bad guys will, and they will be the winners for it. Events from the U.S. border with Mexico recur in this book. The level of criminal violence on the southern side of that border is horrifying. The U.S. Department of Justice identifies 21 distinct narcotraffickers and gang groups that are involved in bringing drugs across the border from Mexico to the United States (National Drug Intelligence Center, 2010, Appendix B4). They supply drugs to over 20,000 criminal groups in the United States for retail sale and distribution (National Drug Intelligence Center, 2010, p. 12). These groups operate not only in areas where the state has little authority today but also in some where it never did. These groups also compete with one another for control over drug supply lines and geography. Their brutality cannot be overstated. As competition escalates and Mexican and U.S. pressure rises, violence is rising and expected to get worse before it gets better (National Drug Intelligence Center, 2010, p. 15).

Moreover, the case of the Hartleys serves as an all-too-vivid example of the current attributes of criminals, let alone their possible future. They make use of the seams in police jurisdictions, in this case the international border. They are trained and brutal, well armed and sophisticated. In Mexico, they outgun the police, if not the army, and their technical capacity for eavesdropping is at least as good. Local police have been a particular Achilles' heel of Mexican law enforcement. The 165,000 municipal officers make up over one-third of the total force (Ellingwood, 2010). They are underpaid—starting salaries in Mexico City in 2002 were as low as $410 per month—undertrained, and ill-equipped, and they lack education beyond the grade-school level (Peters, 2002).

Yet the positive vision of that future is not all that futuristic, for many of the elements are in place today. This book's purpose is to articulate a vision for the future of policing and police forces and to outline steps to make that vision a reality. Some of that vision of the future—for instance, geographical police jurisdictions that less and less accurately match crime's reach across boundaries—has long been with us and will be with us long into the future, but it is not immutable. In other areas, such as technology, much of the future is also already here in terms of potential capacity. A third dimension that will frame the future is also here: Criminals and criminal organizations are adaptive. They will continue to look for seams in public safety defenses, and they will become more and more networked, thus able to learn what works more and more quickly. The three dimensions together—jurisdiction, technology, and threat—together suggest very different concepts of police operations, some of which also are here today, in part. This book intends to put the elements together in a way that can lead to action—by police departments, by citizens, and by private sector organizations.

To be sure, while policing can be dangerous, much of it is boring but necessary, and much of it is intensely local—dealing with traffic accidents, mentally unstable people acting out in public, drunk drivers, and bar fights. This book is focused on major organized crime that is not purely local. Yet, this book's starting point is that such terms as *major*, *organized*, and *local* are changing. Individuals or small groups can now commit major crimes, and global networks mean that local events can have distant roots or effects. Technology can enable new concepts of police operations even for what are very local operations: Suppose that the customer service representative had been en route to a domestic dispute, perhaps the most unpredictably dangerous instance an officer faces. She would surely like her briefing from the database to tell her of previous incidents, what weapons were used, and the like.

Thinking About and Responding to Threats

Criminals and criminal organizations do pose a threat to society. However, it is worth noting the nature of the threat they pose and locating it against other threats to U.S. society and well-being. If *threat* is conceived broadly, then threats can be thought of as covering a range. At one end of the range are those threats that come with threateners attached, people who mean us harm (Treverton, 2001a, pp. 43–46)—purposive threats. At the other end are developments that "can be thought of as *threats without threateners*. The threat results from the cumulative effect of actions taken for other reasons, not from an intent that is purposeful and hostile. [They might also be called *systemic threats*.] Those who burn the Amazon rain forests or try to migrate here or who spread pandemics here . . . do not necessarily wish Americans harm; they simply want to survive or get rich. *Their* self-interest becomes a threat to *us*" (Treverton, 2001b). Figure 1.1 displays the continuum.

Organized crime and drug traffickers fall somewhere in the middle of that continuum. The activities of both harm society and create threats, even ones that might, in some instances—e.g., drug trafficking in Mexico—become ones of concern to national security. Yet, the threateners do not start by intending us harm. Rather, the threat arises as a by-product of their main goal, which is to make themselves rich. They may harm people by selling them dangerous products, like drugs, but those products are ones that their purchasers want, whether or not they should. Other harm results from the way they do business—protecting turf, expanding horizontally or vertically, and so on.

Most of the harm is directed at fellow criminals, but ordinary citizens—not to mention authorities—often get caught in the crossfire. Indeed, criminals want nothing from police—merely to be left alone to commit their crimes. From the criminals' perspectives, if authorities have to be neutralized, it is better to buy them than to fight them. All of this gives rise to the following paradox, one again so painfully

Figure 1.1
From Purposive Threats to Threats Without Threateners

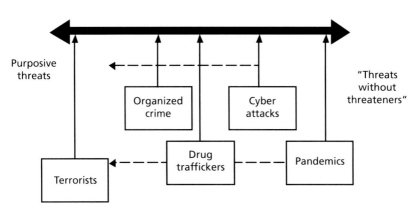

NOTE: The dotted lines leftward from both cyber attacks and pandemics indicate that both could result either from accident or Mother Nature, on the one hand, or, on the other, from purposive foes.

RAND *MG1102-1.1*

on display in northern Mexico: The more harshly authorities seek to repress crime, the greater the harm to citizens and society, at least in the short run. Outbursts of increased violence can arise for other reasons, such as gangs competing for supply lines or turf. But heavier repression is likely—again, in the short run—to lead to more violence and more citizens caught in the crossfire.

What is striking about Figure 1.1 is that the threats at the ends of the continuum are now more important than they were before, especially during the Cold War. If such transnational threats as organized crime were secondary, now another transnational threat, terrorism, is primary. Islamic extremist terrorism is at the purposive end of the threat continuum—i.e., they mean us harm. While terrorism by Islamic extremists does not pose the existential threat to the United States that the Soviet Union and its nuclear weapons did, it is more than an inconvenience. Only pandemics, at the other end of the continuum, pose an existential threat to U.S. society.

The terrorist threat is at the edge of this book's subject. The fight—let alone "war"—against terrorism does not conjure up policing as we usually think of it: cops on the beat deterring crime by their presence and responding to it when it occurs. Yet, in fact, the tools and techniques of law enforcement are very relevant to stopping terror, one of several reasons why calling the effort a "war" is a mistake. Even those officers on the beat are distinctly relevant, for they are eyes and ears in the fight. They are looking not so much for crimes as for anomalies that might begin to unravel a skein leading to intended terrorism. For example, taking pictures of buildings is not a crime and should not be construed as one. But it might be an anomaly worth noting, one that might in combination with other information begin that unraveling.[1]

Terrorism frightens Americans well beyond its actual harm so far. For instance, as a RAND monograph on reorganizing domestic intelligence explains, "polls taken immediately after the September 11 attacks asking how concerned respondents were about more terrorist attacks in the United States recorded 49 percent as worrying 'a great deal' and 38 percent worrying 'somewhat.' Two years later, the proportion worrying 'a great deal' had fallen to 25 percent, whereas the percentage reporting that they were 'somewhat' concerned had risen to 46" (Treverton, 2008, pp. 11–12; American Enterprise Institute for Public Policy Research, 2005). In fact, the loss of life on September 11 was off the charts of America's historical experience with terrorism. In the years after 2001, the yearly numbers of fatalities of Americans from terrorism, worldwide, were all less than 100, and usually barely into double digits (excluding the wars in Iraq and Afghanistan). The total for 2009 was 23, including the 13 killed by Army Major Nidal Hassan at Fort Hood, Texas (National Counterterrorism Center, 2010; U.S. Department of State, undated). That compares with an average over the five years following the September 11 attacks of 62 people per year killed by lightning, 63 from tornadoes, 692 in bike accidents, and a whopping 41,616 in motor vehicle–related accidents.

Yet, if terrorism is thus far not very lethal for Americans, it certainly does get their attention. Figure 1.2 drives home that point by

---

[1] For a thoughtful critique of counterterrorism policy since September 11, 2001, and a strong argument for why law enforcement is better suited for the lead role in stanching terrorism (i.e., terrorists exist at the community level, often funding their activity through criminal enterprises that are the purview of law enforcement), see Bayer, 2010.

Figure 1.2
U.S. Fatalities from Terrorism, Including Iraq, and Press Mentions of al Qaeda

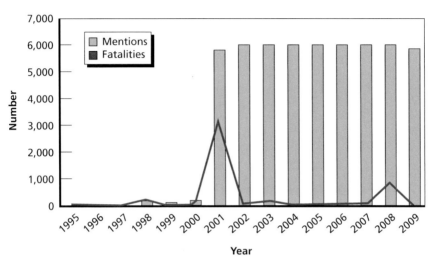

SOURCES: For the number of fatalities: RAND Database of Worldwide Terrorism Incidents; for mentions in the press: LexisNexis Academic, "Major World Publications Category," from January 1 of each year to December 31.
NOTE: The number of mentions accounts for two spellings: "Al-Qaeda" and "Al-Qaida." Between 2002 and 2008, LexisNexis was unable to generate an exact number because that number exceeded 3,000 for both spellings. The number of mentions in those years should therefore be understood as more than 6,000.
RAND MG1102-1.2

comparing mentions of al Qaeda in global publications to fatalities from terrorism, including U.S. soldiers in Iraq. Fatalities spiked and then dropped, but attention to al Qaeda remained high. In that sense, the threat of terrorism makes the vision of future policing set out here more vivid, and perhaps more actionable, than would otherwise be the case. Reshaping policing and law enforcement more generally to deal with terrorism moves both areas in the direction that this book's vision for the future implies. It means making more and better use of technologies. Because the goal of counterterrorism is prevention before the fact, not enforcement afterward, it needs to be driven by intelligence. So is the broader vision of policing set out here. In addition, changes in both technology and task call for new concepts of operations.

In some ways, the kinship between the fight against terror and policing techniques is obscured by the language we use. "Law enforcement" does conjure up that vision of cops on the beat, deterring if they can but mostly there to catch bad guys after they behave badly. In fact, catching bad guys is a way station, or "output," to what we really care about, which is preventing crime. Catching criminals is supposed to reduce crime in two ways—by taking likely repeat criminals off the street and by deterring others who might follow in their footsteps. Yet, for both terrorism and crime, the ultimate goal—the outcome that society seeks—is nothing: no terrorist attacks and no crime. The difference is one more of magnitude than of kind: Because terrorism is so scary and because it can be horrific, the rhetoric of our politicians suggests, unrealistically, that we must absolutely prevent it. By contrast, while crime can be horrific, much of it can be tolerated: If we don't get the perpetrators this time, we will the next.

For this reason, and because of that cop-on-the-beat vision of policing, it is all too easy to mix up ends and means, or what economists call inputs, outputs, and outcomes (Wilson and Cox, 2008). Outcomes are what we ultimately care about. They are states of society. A crime rate is close to an outcome, for it measures how much society is harmed by crime. In many respects, we might prefer a "safety index," a positive measure, to a negative one, a crime rate. Crimes, somehow weighted for their severity, would then lower that index.

Crime rates are almost an outcome, for they capture only what the accounting system can capture; if unreported crimes remain invisible, they are neglected. Thus, assuming that reporting and accounting systems remain the same from one year to the next, crime rates are probably pretty accurate in relative terms: Was there more of a particular crime this year than last? However, because what goes unreported remains unknown, they are not especially good as measures of the safety index.

At the other end of the means-ends spectrum is inputs. These are the means of policing—the number of police officers, their level of training, the number of cars, the pattern in which they are deployed, the number of specialized units, and so on. Again, that cop-on-the-beat image sometimes makes it seem that inputs are ends in themselves. They are not. They are only inputs. If more cops on the street do not have any visible effect, their addition is only an employment program. What inputs should affect are outputs—the results of combining the inputs in particular ways. For policing, the most common outputs are quantitative: cases or arrests. Connecting inputs to outputs seems straightforward and often is. If employing more police did not lead to more arrests, there would be grounds for suspicion. But suppose an input were directly connected to an outcome—if, for instance, people were reassured by the presence of more police, whether or not those police caught more criminals (an output) or reduced the crime rate (a near outcome).

Not surprisingly, the challenge is connecting outputs to outcomes. Take crime rates. If placing more police on the street is followed by a decrease in crime rates, it is plausible to connect the two. But it is not convincing, for so many other factors bear on the crime rate. Aging populations, for instance, commit less crime, and crime is also affected by other demographic changes. The state of the economy may have an effect. So may the state of workfare or other social welfare programs. Making the case convincingly requires assessments rooted in quasi-experimental studies (Heaton, 2010). What is critical in the pages that follow is to keep in mind that means and ends in policing are not the same things, and that what matters most are ends, those outcomes in society that we seek to advance with better policing.

Plan of This Book

Chapter Two provides a snapshot of policing today, as well as background on how we got there. It aims to describe what exists already, rather than to make judgments. It recognizes and builds on the work and debate that has gone on. For instance, the Society of Police Futurists International and the Federal Bureau of Investigation's (FBI's) Futures Working Group are both small but have been thinking along some similar lines. They have also looked at future demographics, such as declining birthrates in developed countries; "youth bulges" in at-risk countries and failed states; "senior bulges" in the developed world;

huge patterns of immigration, legal and otherwise; and future technologies, such as nanotechnology and augmented reality (Futures Working Group, undated; Police Futurists International, 2002; see also Cetron and Davies, 2008).

Chapter Two lays out, somewhat schematically, four phases in the modern history of policing—the political era (from the 1840s to the early 1900s), the reform era (from the 1930s to the late 1970s), the community era (from the 1980s to the present day), and the intelligence era, beginning with September 11, 2001 (Stewart and Morris, 2009, p. 291). The categories are not neat, and the eras overlap. For instance, ILP developed in England in the 1980s. It shared the focus on intelligence of the current era, but its purpose was different: It sought to better anticipate crime and thus save money by deploying fewer of those cops on the beat. Yet, the eras serve as a reminder that the paradigm of policing has changed in the past and, thus, could and will change again. The overlap is a caution that the shift will not be swift—perhaps not fast enough.

The chapter concludes with the first mismatch between police organization and crime. Police forces typically are comprised of both geographic and functional units, and each is jealous of its turf. Who is in charge of a particular investigation is often an issue. Intelligence can be a particular stepchild in the system. Some departments have intelligence analysts but not crime analysts; others are the reverse. Even when a department has both, they are quite different disciplines and may not communicate well with each other. Senior officers in the department too seldom get both detailed crime statistics and a broader picture of threats within the department's domain.

Chapter Three turns to jurisdiction. Policing is mismatched to crime, for it is still primarily organized by geography, while crime is not. The bank robbed in a cyber crime may be in New York, but the criminals may be in Estonia, operating through a half dozen computers they have commandeered in six different parts of the globe. The Los Angeles region is a poster child for the mismatch at the next level up from individual police departments: between services. Santa Monica is surrounded by Los Angeles but has its own police force. Yet, most sharing of information is driven by particular crimes; routine sharing is rare. In addition, as late as 2009, Santa Monica had different communication networks than Culver City, five miles away, and so found communication difficult.

These sources of mismatch are deeply rooted in not only the culture of policing but also the nature of American society in which police forces are embedded. For all the mystique that the FBI has created around itself over the years, its agents account for only 2 percent of the nation's sworn officers. Yet, the nation's Jeffersonian ethos would oppose a full national police force even if it could be shown convincingly that such a force would reduce crime significantly. If working across borders within a single metropolitan region is hard, imagine working across international borders. The U.S.-Mexico border is a stark example, for it becomes as much a seam in police defenses, and a sanctuary for criminals, as it is a protection. Efforts to work around the various mismatches are mostly ad hoc and are driven by operational needs. Cooperation is at the service-to-service level in particular cases. More-formal efforts at cooperation are still works in progress, like the U.S. fusion centers, or are weak, like Interpol.

Chapter Four turns to technology. Two features of technology and policing are striking. The first is that, until recently, the innovations that changed policing the most—from automobiles to telephones to computers—were not invented for police or to improve policing. Rather, they were invented to make everyday life easier or richer. The second is that whatever technologies the police employ, the criminals can too. The key to the future of policing, then, is not technology but the ways that police forces adapt it to their purposes. At its core, technology has the potential to change (1) data and intelligence gathering, (2) problem-solving processes, (3) partnership structures, and (4) departmental organization. Chapter Four examines those dimensions in turn, after emphasizing the importance of changing concepts of operations (ConOps) to make the most of new technology and taking a look backward at technology's role in making policing what it is today.

Chapter Five takes up the changing threat. The globalization of commerce and technology has helped to fundamentally alter the nature of the threat to society from crime. The threat will continue to morph. Criminals are now committing crimes, such as identity theft, from home that previously required teams of people and intense coordination. Individuals and small groups can commit major crimes and thus are changing what "organized crime" means. Technology-enabled crime has arrived and will continue to develop. And the next step, "virtual" crimes, is not far off; already there are harbingers of that new arena of crime. At the same time, "old" crimes are evolving as to be almost completely distinct from the real-world crimes from which they emerged. In addition, the environment in which criminals operate will morph as technology, law, and law enforcement change. None of these dimensions operates independently of one another; they are all interconnected in complex ways.

Chapter Six turns to concepts of operations, or ConOps. Technology can enable, but to make a difference it must be incorporated in changes in how police organizations go about their business. For instance, new technologies to build and search databases are an opportunity, but taking advantage of those technologies requires a different skill set than that of most police officers. It requires analysts, and it is likely to shift the balance on the force away from sworn officers toward civilians. Money is often viewed as a constraint in developing new approaches to operations, all the more so given the budgetary straits in which American cities find themselves. But it can be an incentive to be creative with new ConOps. Departments are finding ways to use more civilians, both because of the skill sets they bring and because they can be cheaper than officers. For similar reasons, new partnerships in new areas of policing between police and private companies are also on the agenda. So, too, the process of responding to a changed and changing threat is compelling police to find new ways to work across the seams in jurisdiction.

Changes in policing are almost certain to raise concerns over privacy and other civil liberties. That is a lesson of policing's history. Concerns will be sharper for techniques that seem more intrusive and are more likely to involve innocent bystanders; witness the opposition to data mining. But people also want to be safe, so if effectiveness can be demonstrated—via evidence-based policing—concerns will be diminished. So far there have been reactions in particular places to specific innovations in police practice—like ubiquitous cameras—but no broad public backlash against innovation in policing.

The concluding chapter, Chapter Seven, begins by summing up the vision of policing in the future, across the three categories of technology, threat, and jurisdiction. The point, however, is not to let the best be the enemy of the good and still less to convey the impression that until everything changes, nothing can. The chapter thus concludes with a menu of concrete and doable steps that police organizations can take to move toward that positive vision of the future.

CHAPTER TWO

Policing Today

As our friend and colleague, Lt. John Sullivan of the Los Angeles Sheriff's Department, puts it,

> In many ways, film and video capture the cop's life better than written text. For me Barney Miller was just about right in my appreciation of the day-to-day feelings. . . . Police work is routine, mundane boredom, punctuated by sheer terror, mayhem, crisis, excitement, and bureaucratic blunder. On top of this add valor, compassion, and drama. It strikes at the core of human life and experience (in all weather) . . . .

Film may be more graphic, but cops writing about their craft also convey Sullivan's combination of boredom and terror. Here is one portrayal from a high-crime area in Brooklyn:

> In the ghetto, this is the way it works. You pull up to a drug location at three in the morning and toss [search] the dealer, steerer, banker and look-out under the Right of Common Inquiry. Why? Because they've disrespected you by not "stepping off" (walking away) when you drove by. You know they're running a drug operation, and they know you know. And the respect they should show is to curtail business for forty seconds at the sight of you. And if they don't then you stop the car, get out, and toss them. And it's, "Yo! [expletive], take your hands out of your [expletive] pockets and get on the fall. Don't even [expletive] look at me."
> . . . [W]hat you're trying to do is program them into "getting

it." *When I pull up to this corner, you walk.* (Poss and Schlesinger, 2002, p. 5)

Understanding the historical trajectory of the American policing system is necessary to fully comprehend policing practices today. Kelling and Moore (1988) identified three eras of policing—political, reform, and community. Since then, those three have been supplemented by a fourth category, intelligence-based policing (Stewart and Morris, 2009). These classifications represent paradigm shifts in the organization, goals, and tactics of American police forces. To be sure, the categories are neither neat nor neatly separated in time. They overlap, and each has spawned variants. The intelligence-based policing era has recently resurfaced, and much of policing today is characteristic of the community-policing era. Goals during the current period include order maintenance and crime control. Tactics consist of many variants of deterrence through presence, increased communication with the community, and heightened stringency of punishment. While the discussions of the eras and tactics, inputs and outputs, and goals and outcomes all overlap, this chapter artificially separates these concepts in an effort to be clear and inclusive of the existing concepts in the history of policing.

The Political Era

In 1927, Herbert Asbury wrote *The Gangs of New York*, a stylized historical exposé of the notorious Five Points neighborhood in ante- and post-bellum New York City (Asbury, 1927). The book features immigrant gangs who not only exert their own brand of community policing but also were often members of the police force and civil servants themselves. Policing practices remained guided by the law, but the mutually beneficial relationship between the policing force and politicians resulted in high levels of corruption—hardly surprisingly. Police encouraged citizens to vote for specific candidates and helped rig elections while politicians both helped recruit and maintain the police in the office and on the beat.

Corruption in police departments spurred the response in the Reform Era to depoliticize the police and other civil services. While it may be an overstatement to call all police departments of the political era corrupt, surely that era was characterized by various shades of clientelism. Police departments were political structures, politicians used police departments to garner local political influence, police officers were themselves elected at high levels, and many people joined the police department in order to advance political careers down the line. As a result, police departments catered to their voters. On the extreme end of the spectrum, a position as a police officer in New York's Tammany Hall could be bought for $300 with no special training or knowledge required. The fact that few measures of accountability went with positions only increased temptations toward corruption and nepotism (Walker, 1999, p. 24).

In the political era, limitations in both authority and technology meant that policing was localized in neighborhoods or communities, even within larger cities. Cultural references to this era of policing evoke images of the local foot patrolman, involved in daily neighborhood activities. Citizens made complaints in person at the local police station, and the police force was closely tied to those under their jurisdiction (Reiss, 1992). However, Walker (1999) suggests that the image of the friendly, knowledgeable neighborhood constable is misleading, notwithstanding the localization of policing within communities. Police turnover was high, and officers often did not have enough time to get to know the neighborhoods they patrolled.

Unlike the British police force, which was given central authority from the crown, the American police primarily gained legitimacy from local political leaders. Because of the competition between the two major parties, police were focused on providing a wide variety of services to the community in addition to crime prevention and order maintenance (Kelling and Moore, 1988). These services included running soup lines and providing temporary lodging or finding work for immigrant workers or displaced and wayward youths. In addition, evidence from Boston indicates that officers also served public health functions by checking households daily for cholera outbreaks (Whitehouse, 1973).

The Reform Era

As Americans grew frustrated with the level of corruption within their police forces, pressures to restructure the organization and practices of the police resulted in what is now known as the reform era of policing (Kelling and Moore, 1988). Using as a model J. Edgar Hoover's successful efforts to restructure and rebrand the FBI, O. W. Wilson, the Chicago police chief, attempted to transform American police agencies to make them legitimate and remove them from political pressures. William Parker was doing the same for Los Angeles at about the same time. Police were pulled out of the community and disconnected so that corruption was less likely to develop. In the process, the scope of policing narrowed from the provision of broad community social services to a focus on law enforcement. The force became "professionalized"—approaching crime prevention and criminal apprehension from an objective and strategic standpoint. As a reaction to the disillusionment with the political policing era, the reform era withdrew police from community involvement almost entirely, focusing singularly on policing and investigative activities. Police forces made efforts to be objective in their criminal prevention and apprehension practices. This included beginning attempts to standardize policing practices while decreasing subjective judgment calls of individual officers.

In 1924, Attorney General Harlan Fiske Stone appointed J. Edgar Hoover as the director of the FBI (Jeffreys-Jones, 2007). Using Scotland Yard as a model, Stone directed Hoover to purge the agency of unreliable staff and recruit personnel of good character with legal training. Although Hoover's hiring practices were and continued to be controversial, the conservative dress code, fidelity, and general moral code established in the handbook of conduct that Hoover distributed within weeks of his appointment created a uniform workforce culture. The FBI also restricted its investigations to criminal activities, refraining from the much more political investigations of such organizations as the Women's League for Peace and Freedom that had characterized the agency's past. From 1929 to 1931, Attorney General George W. Wickersham chaired a federal commission that exposed policing practices that undermined public confidence, including but not limited to "third-degree" interrogations. Hoover also attempted to professionalize the FBI's practices and directed FBI agents to avoid political activities and the overuse of firearms. These practices reinforced the FBI as an investigative agency, distinct from the political and corrupt police forces of the previous era.

In 1930, Congress authorized the FBI to begin collecting criminal data and statistics, and Hoover attempted to improve the effectiveness of policing practices and crime detection. "Uniform crime reporting" established the categories within the American major crime index: murder, rape, robbery, serious assault, larceny, burglary, and auto theft. In 1932, Hoover established a laboratory for ballistics, fiber analysis, chemical analysis of blood, and other technical capabilities. In addition, he centralized and took control over the national fingerprinting files. In 1933, the new attorney general, Homer S. Cummings, labeled America's police force the best in the world in a radio broadcast. In April 1934, Cummings announced the enactment of 21 laws that defined and created interstate crimes over which the agency would now have jurisdiction, gave FBI agents the power to make arrests and carry arms, and tightened the rules even further on personnel recruitment.

Politically, police forces became more autonomous and less accountable to local politicians and public pressures. At the same time, technological developments not only increased the capacity of the police to respond to crime but also distanced officers from their respective communities. Tactical strategies revolved around preventive patrol and rapid response. The quickly moving patrol car supplanted the slower practice of foot patrol as the major form of police presence. Kelling and Moore write, "It represented mobility, power, conspicuous presence, control of officers, and professional distance from citizens" (1988, p. 8). Other developments, such as the incorporation of radio and telephone in the force, also enabled policing to react more quickly (Reiss, 1992). The increased capacity for communication led to the centralization of command organization and force mobilization within jurisdictions. Because the police could now respond quickly to calls of distress, the deployment of specialized squads and bureaus replaced the local patrolman. This paradigm shift led to an increased demand in the policing labor market—with expert teams requiring at least twice as many officers as the traditional foot-beat system.

None of this is to imply that police departments were always eager for change or that they passively accepted attempts to bring more transparency and accountability into policing structures. In 1937, the home of Clinton Clifford, a shop owner in Los Angeles and an avid campaigner for reform within the Los Angeles Police Department, was bombed in an attempt to silence his inquiries into the levels of corruption in City Hall and the police department. The next year, the car of an investigator with whom Clifford was working, Harry Raymond, was also bombed. Two Los Angeles police officers were convicted in the bombing ("California: Reform Over Los Angeles," 1938).

Although policing did transform across the country, the reform era model soon proved incapable of dealing with rapid changes in American society. First, in spite of the improvements made to force structure and policing strategies and tactics, crime did not decrease. In fact, as Figure 2.1 shows, the 1960s saw an increase in the level of

Figure 2.1
Homicide Rates, 1950–1990

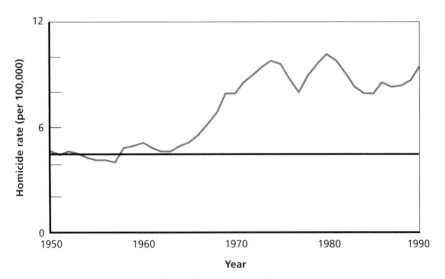

SOURCE: Derived from FBI Uniform Crime Reports (FBI, undated[a]).
RAND MG1102-2.1

crimes and fear, calling into question the effectiveness of policing in general.

To be sure, recent studies have examined the spike in crime and provided a number of possible explanations in addition to the failure of reform-era policing. Still, the increase in crime did diminish the faith of the public in police reforms at the time. In fact, the reform era's focus on research as an aid to objectivity and the improvement of police practices ultimately proved that the reforms were not necessarily successful.

Research suggested that neither preventive patrol nor rapid response was very effective. In 1972, the Police Foundation (an operating group, not a philanthropic foundation) collaborated with the police department in Kansas City, Missouri, to undertake a large experiment to test and analyze the effectiveness of preventive police patrolling. The experiment divided the 15 Kansas City police beats into three groups and varied the level of routine preventive patrol within them. In the "control" beats, preventive patrol was maintained at its current level of one patrol car per beat; in the "reactive" beats, preventive patrol was eliminated, and officers only responded to calls for service; in the "proactive" beats, routine patrol increased to two or three times the regular level. The Kansas City Preventive Patrol Experiment hypothesized that crime, citizen perception of police services, and citizen fear and fear-based behavior would not increase by patrol type, but that both response time and satisfaction would vary by patrol group, and that traffic accidents would escalate in the "reactive" beats (Kelling, Pate, Dieckman, and Brown, 1974).

There turned out to be very little difference between patrol patterns—"experimental conditions"—on any dimension, thus undercutting faith in preventive patrol. The summary report of the experiment listed the following findings:

- "[A]s revealed in the victimization surveys, the experimental conditions had no significant effect on residence and non-residence burglaries, auto thefts, larcenies involving auto accessories, robberies, or vandalism—crimes traditionally considered to be deterrable through preventive patrol;

- in terms of rates of reporting crime to the police, few differences and no consistent patterns of differences occurred across experimental conditions;
- in terms of departmental reported crime, only one set of differences across experimental conditions was found, and it was judged likely to have been a random occurrence.
- few significant differences and no consistent pattern of differences were discovered across experimental conditions in terms of citizen attitudes toward police services;
- citizen fear of crime, overall, was not affected by experimental conditions;
- there were few differences and no consistent pattern of differences across experimental conditions in the number and types of anti-crime protective measures used by citizens;
- in general, the attitudes of businessmen toward crime and police services were not affected by experimental conditions;
- experimental conditions did not appear to significantly affect citizen satisfaction with the police as a result of their encounters with police officers;
- experimental conditions had no significant effect on either police response time or citizen satisfaction with police response time;
- although few measures were used to assess the impact of experimental conditions on traffic accidents and injuries, no significant differences were apparent;
- about 60 percent of a police officer's time is typically uncommitted and thus available for calls; of this time, police officers spent approximately as much time on non-police related activities as they did on police-related mobile patrol; and
- in general, police officers are given neither a uniform definition of preventive patrol nor any objective methods for gauging its effectiveness; while officers tend to be ambivalent in their estimates of preventive patrol's effectiveness in deterring crime, many attach great importance to preventive patrol as a police function" (Kelling, Pate, Dieckman, and Brown, 1974, p. 3).

Although the experiment did not address other issues related to police patrol, such as team policing or generalist-specialist models, the scale of the project and its findings generated powerful ripples among both police departments around the United States and the American public.

At the same time, issues of racial and gender discrimination were boiling up on the political agenda, and this further increased the disillusionment with the so-called "objective" policing practices of the reform era, at least for many of America's citizens. The 1960s saw an increase in protests and riots, which, by their nature, pitted groups of the public against the police—the symbol of control and order. As a result, the police became the enemy of segments of the American population.

The police in this era, however, were not always merely innocent victims of a public backlash. In 1968, the *Detroit Free Press* released survey results that outlined blacks' perceived problems in the months before the July 1967 riots. Their number one concern was police brutality (Jeffries, 2010, p. 133). The "Big Four" or "Tac Squads," elite four-man police units, aggressively policed the Detroit neighborhoods. Blacks tended to see them as antagonistic and exacerbating the racial tensions at the time. These social tensions culminated in the Detroit riot of 1967, a violent demonstration in reaction to a police raid on a party for two returning Vietnam War veterans. "Within 48 hours, the National Guard was mobilized, to be followed by the 82nd Airborne Division on the riot's fourth day" ("The Detroit Riots of 1967: Events," undated). At the end of the five-day riot, 43 were dead, 1,189 had been injured, and over 7,000 had been arrested. These trends would continue around the country as well. Following the widely publicized Kent State massacre in May 1970, the Jackson State killings in 1970 of four college student protesters also caused a backlash against police practices.

It became evident that the policing practices of the reform era were ill-equipped to handle the changing political and social dynamics in the United States. In its place, what developed were the concepts of the community era that continue to underlie current policing practices.

The Community Era

A police officer working the downtown area of a major urban center walks into a local coffee house on her beat. She smiles at the manager, who starts making her usual order, and inquires after goings-on in the neighborhood. It turns out that the bookseller across the street has been vandalized, and the officer asks if anyone saw anything suspicious in the area last night. As the officer pays for her coffee, the manager says that he noticed something while he was doing inventory last night. The coffee shop's security camera has a partial view of the bookseller, and maybe the camera has caught something of value. A quick replay of the security tape from last night reveals that two youths were loitering near where the vandalism occurred. The officer notes a description of the youths and uses her BlackBerry to upload a message to the department's Twitter feed with information about the suspects, requesting information from citizens who subscribe to the department's feed. Wishing the manager a good day, the officer steps back onto the street and continues the patrol of her beat.

Much of the story outlined above is typical of the classic community-based policing model. An officer who regularly patrols the area and knows the community members well engages citizens to build trust and cooperation in order to solve the community's safety problems. The community-based policing model developed in large measure as a reaction to the increasing use of new technologies in police departments. The patrol car took officers off the streets and thus decreased the face-to-face interaction with the people they were serving. Advanced phone systems allowed for greater problem-handling via telephone instead of community members coming into the station. These advances are neither good nor bad; as with almost all change, there are trade-offs and adjustments. However, they did have the result of distancing the police from the community during the reform era. As a result, the community era has sought to reestablish a closer connection between the police force and surrounding community (Kelling and Moore, 1988).

Despite the negative media attention that police forces received at the end of the reform era, studies in the 1970s showed both that the public appreciates foot patrolling and that information provided by the community could be useful in curbing crime. These developments have led to problem-oriented policing, an approach of the community era that takes a holistic view of the crime in a community. Instead of viewing each criminal incident as an isolated event, policing seeks to discern broader patterns and to address underlying factors. The goal of policing has once again broadened beyond merely controlling crime; community-based policing focuses on the prevention of crime as well. The lineage of community-based policing today can be traced back to Sir Robert Peel's reforms of the London police department in the 1830s. At that time, Peel also implemented the paramilitary command structure of the police department that is ubiquitous in policing today. He reasoned that while civilian control was paramount, only lines of command and discipline similar to those of the military could provide police with the incentive to properly patrol and enforce the law on their beats in London's rough streets—something that night watchmen of the time could not be persuaded to do.

Community-based policing today emphasizes good relations with local communities as a means both of gaining good intelligence and, perhaps, of enlisting community leaders as would-be deterrents. This strategy is characterized by three primary aspects: citizen input, broad functions, and personal service (Gordner, 1996; Greene, 1987, pp. 1–16). Seeking the input of ordinary citizens not only provides additional support for implementing policing strategies but also confers local police with greater authority and legitimacy. Techniques used in this regard include creating various advisory boards, conducting community polls, and holding town meetings, along with other formal channels for communication between the police force and the target community. The second characteristic of community-based policing speaks to the expanded role of the modern police force. In addition to trying to prevent specific criminal events, community-based policing works more generally with residents to establish safe environments. This emphasis on services ranges from traffic safet, to decreased drug abuse, fear reduction, and support for victims of domestic violence. The last characteristic of community-based policing is an emphasis on the personal service of the force, again a reaction to the approach of the reform era, which was perceived to be bureaucratic and removed from the people served.

Common policing practices today that emphasize the community relationship and a discerning problem-solving approach include foot and other forms of patrol, directed and differential patrol approaches, and case screening. While foot patrols can improve the community's view of the police and reduce fear, whether they actually prevent crime has been an open question since the 1980s. Following in the footsteps of the Kansas City Preventive Patrol Experiment, a number of studies have been tasked with understanding the effectiveness of community-based policing and have so far produced mixed results. The Druid Hills experiment in Birmingham, Alabama, revealed that involving the local community in preventing and controlling crime through such efforts as door-to-door visits and town meetings did have an impact on the number of calls received by the police reporting violent crimes (Kessler and Borella, 1997, pp. 95–115.).

In contrast, studies and experiments based in Newark, Boston, and Houston found that foot patrol had no significant effect on crime (Kelling, Pate, Dieckman, and Brown, 1974; Kessler and Duncan, 1996). At the same time, studies in Michigan and Baltimore found the opposite—that crime had decreased 8.7 percent and 12 percent, respectively (Trojanowicz and Belknap, 1986; Cordner, 1988). In addition, a more recent experiment in Philadelphia, which involved a randomized controlled trial, found that foot patrols decreased crime by 23 percent (Ratcliffe, Groff, Wood, Taniguchi, Johnson, Taylor, Sorg, and Haberman, 2011).

The debate over effectiveness extends beyond foot patrol and community involvement, however, and many of the concepts involved warrant further discussion. These include order-maintenance policing (OMP) to control the environmental influencers of crime, the idea of deterrence through presence, the use of directed patrol to reduce crime in criminal "hot spots," and a problem-solving approach to crime.

Order-Maintenance Policing

OMP is the subject of many studies and much academic debate in the policing world. In 1982, James Q. Wilson and George Kelling published "Broken Windows," a study that would transform the practices of policing for decades to come (Kelling and Wilson, 1982). They posited that "fixing broken windows," or preventing public disorder, would not only establish a norm against crime in a neighborhood but would also convey to the public that the police was invested in the community. The result was OMP—or the control of the social influences of crime to restrain overall criminal activity. By targeting such minor infractions as vagrancy, littering, graffiti, vandalism, and public intoxication, the police could control the environmental influences that enabled more serious offenses. Although the final outcome would be a reduction in crime, the tactical goal of the police was to maintain order within a community.

Because both aggressive OMP and computer statistics (CompStat) are associated with William Bratton's time as police commissioner in New York City, the two are often linked. But CompStat can be seen as the transition from community policing to intelligence-led policing (ILP). The brainchild of the now-legendary Jack Maple, who Bratton elevated from lieutenant to deputy commissioner, the process began by tracking crime in the New York subway system on large wall maps. Maple called the maps "charts of the future." When they were computerized, CompStat was born, and "precinct commanders were held accountable for crimes in their area. For the first time that anyone could remember, crime in New York City began to decline" (Dussault, 1999; see Figure 2.2).

As it developed, CompStat became "a process by which crime statistics are collected, computerized, mapped and disseminated quickly" (Dussault, 1999). While local commanders are responsible for choosing strategy and are then held responsible for those choices, Bratton did emphasize quality of life offenses, giving officers latitude to aggressively target and arrest violators for such behaviors as public drunkenness, vandalism, minor drug use, excessive noise, and other similar behaviors. Bratton and others credited the combination of quality of life strategy and CompStat's practices for the large decrease in crime in the city at the time (Rosenfeld, Fornango, and Rengifo, 2007).

Not surprisingly, given the history of policing, Bratton's assertions about both OMP and CompStat drew skepticism in the form

Figure 2.2
New York City Violent Crime Rates, 1985–2000

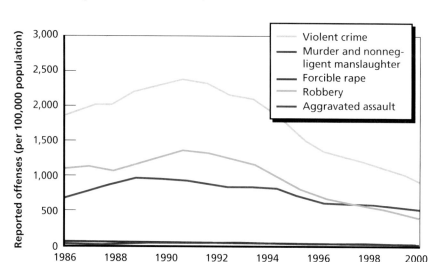

SOURCES: FBI, Uniform Crime Reports, prepared by the National Archive of Criminal Justice Data.
RAND MG1102-2.2

of empirical studies to test the effectiveness of OMP. To this day, the OMP initiative, as well as the underlying theory supporting OMP, has continued to be the subject of much debate. Empirical papers have resulted in a wide range of conclusions. Some studies have found that "broken-windows policing" led to decreases in violent crime (Kelling and Sousa, 2001; Rosenfeld, Fornango, and Rengifo, 2007), and six field experiments in a randomized Dutch study found evidence that when people see that norms or rules have been violated, they are more likely to do so themselves (Keizer, Lindenberg, and Steg, 2008). Other studies have concluded, more tentatively, that CompStat may have been at least partially responsible for the decreases in crime (Karmen, 2000; Conklin, 2003). However, still others attribute the fall in New York's criminal activity to a variety of other factors, including the decrease of crime nationwide (Harcourt, 2001; Joanes, 2000; Fagan, Zimring, and Kim, 1998).

Some of these differences in conclusions about OMP may reflect different empirical methods, but they also reflect the difficulty of isolating the OMP component, especially the simultaneous increase in accountability of the New York police force, which was, after all, the main point of CompStat. As with the studies about the effect of community-based policing, evaluating OMP reflects the devilish challenge of connecting policing inputs and outputs to the outcomes sought— less crime and more safety.

Moreover, OMP has spawned its own backlash, one akin to that during the reform era. Social advocates continued to question the equity of policing practices even in the era of community policing. These critics of OMP believe that it serves as a justification and "cover for the surveillance of 'disorderly people,' often young minority males" (Rosenfeld, Fornango, and Rengifo, 2007, p. 357). OMP sometimes influences policing practices today in unexpected ways. In 2008, Flint, Michigan, Police Chief David Dicks instituted a crackdown on baggy pants. This decision was noticed across the United States and generated much controversy, but Dicks held firmly that sagging pants were a form of indecent exposure—something that OMP believes contributes to a supporting environment for crime ("Police Chief: Sag Your Pants, Go to Jail," 2008).

Deterrence Through Presence

Much of policing today is about presence. The presumption is that the presence of blue will not only act as a deterrent but will also shorten response times when crime occurs. Preventive patrol has been the traditional method of increasing the presence of the police force to the public (Klockars, 1983; Skolnick and Bayley, 1986). The underlying theory behind this strategy is based on notions of deterrence, which suggest that the certainty of punishment has a greater impact on changing criminal behavior than the severity of that punishment (Koper, 1995, pp. 649–672; Andenaes, 1974; Blumstein, Cohen, and Nagin, 1978). It follows logically, then, that increasing police presence generally should heighten perceptions of the chances of being apprehended by the police—again, a plausible connection between inputs (more police) and outputs (more arrests).

As with all recent policing strategies, the effectiveness of deterrence through presence has been called into question by different studies. Although many studies, including those of New York City's precincts (Wilson, 1983) and subway system (Chaiken, Lawless, and Stevenson, 1974) and Nashville's patrol zones (Schnelle, Kirchner, Casey, Uselton, and McNees, 1977), have indicated that increasing the tooth-to-tail ratio of law enforcement may have a positive impact (Koper, 1995), Kelling's landmark Kansas City Preventive Patrol Experiment seemed to show the opposite—that variations in motor patrol affected neither crime nor citizens' perceptions of it (Kelling, Pate, Dieckman, and Brown, 1974). Although "the study was criticized on methodological and statistical grounds," the findings gained traction and found support in other studies (Koper, 1995, p. 650; Sherman, 1990, pp. 1–48; Weisburd and Lum, 2005, pp. 419–434). Despite some of these conclusions and the doubts they spawned, deterrence through presence has formed the foundation for a more specific policing tactic: directed patrol.

Directed Patrol and Crackdowns

Directed patrol is a targeted form of deterrence through presence. Its intellectual roots are in what is called "routine activities theory" (Cohen and Felson, 1979), "which holds that crime does not occur randomly but rather is produced by the convergence in time and space of motivated offenders, suitable targets, and the absence of capable guardians" (Koper, 1995, p. 652). The combination of all these factors creates hot spots of crime (Kessler and Borella, 1997). Although simply displacing these crimes to another location is a concern, these new locations may not possess all the characteristics of a hot spot and thus may be less conducive to serious crime. Another possible outcome is that the crime may be displaced to a time with fewer potential victims.

This theory has formed the foundation for directed patrol projects and police crackdowns, which are defined as "increases in either the certainty or severity of official police reaction to a specific type of crime or all crime in a specific area. . . . Police crackdowns constitute a sudden, usually proactive change in activity" (Sherman, 1990). A variety of experiments and studies have also been undertaken to test the effectiveness of specific deterrence in crime prevention. In 1976, the Police Foundation conducted an experiment in Kansas City to contrast three different policing strategies (Kelling, Pate, Dieckman, and Brown, 1974). Two location-based efforts outperformed the other two approaches, which were offender-based, though the overall impact on crime was indeterminate.

This study was followed by the Kansas City Gun Experiment and a similar initiative conducted in Indianapolis, both of which sought to implement directed patrol. Studies of both programs concluded that they did decrease the amount of gun crimes in the hot spots, though no effect was found on other forms of criminal activity (McGarrell, Chermak, Weiss, and Wilson, 2001). In a study in Lowell, Massachusetts, an experiment found significant reductions in crime and calls for service in hot spots where a disorder policing strategy was employed relative to hot spots that received no special treatment (Braga and Bond, 2008). However, the extent of agreement on the effectiveness of directed patrol is also limited, with other studies discounting the positive relationship found in the studies cited above (Jacob and Rich, 1981; Weiss and Freels, 1996).

Problem-Oriented Policing

All of these approaches—OMP, deterrence through presence, and directed patrol—are improved by the community era's focus on problem-solving. Herman Goldstein's theory of problem-oriented policing (POP), a concept usually discussed in conjunction with community-based policing, calls for "analysis, study, and evaluation" as a necessary precursor to successful law enforcement (Goldstein, 2003, p. 14). POP stresses the need for creative, tailored approaches to crime prevention and also rejects the idea that criminal activities are singular events; rather, it states that most, if not all, crimes can be linked to patterns of behavior over time. Experiments held in Madison, Wisconsin; Baltimore County, Maryland; and Newport News, Virginia, all tested Goldstein's approach. Goldstein and his colleagues discovered in Virginia not only that police enjoyed employing a holistic approach to crime but also that working with the community was effective and simultaneously bolstered public confidence in the police force.

The Intelligence-Led Policing Era

Just as the Kansas City Preventive Patrol Experiment was the stimulus for community policing, the September 11 attacks ushered in a new phase of ILP, a phase that is, in part, back to the future. Because this book's vision of the future is very much in the ILP vein, it is worth pausing over ILP here. One part of ILP is new: the addition of terrorism prevention and response to the tasks of current policing; it is based on the recognition that some targets cannot easily be penetrated through improved police-community relations alone (Ratcliffe, 2008; Carter and Carter, 2009). Because this represents a shift in the goals of policing tactics, ILP has been called a new era of policing by some, particularly in reference to Kelling and Moore's original three eras. For some purposes, understanding the homeland security–focused ILP as a new era distinct from community-based policing makes sense because the addition of new goals to police departments and the accompanying practices to achieve them might entail a shift in focus and resources.

The other part of ILP, though, focuses on developing stronger analytical tools to support policing practices—for which CompStat was the emblem. Although the term ILP is used to discuss both of these concepts (the homeland security aspect and the analytic aspect), they are distinct, and much of the theoretical and practical literature of the two topics does not overlap. From an operational standpoint, scholars have long discussed the need for better information and coordination between agencies. Although the terrorism-focused understanding of ILP includes an emphasis on better data collection and data processing, the analytical-focused understanding of ILP need not include a focus on terrorism at all. In that sense, ILP can be seen as a refinement of community and problem-solving policing.

The origins of ILP go back to England in the 1980s, hence back to the future. Then, it was driven by budget stringency, but it anticipated later evolutions in policing. The term can be traced to the Kent and Northumbria constabularies in particular (McGarrell, Freilich, and Chermak, 2007, p. 144; also see Bureau of Justice Assistance, 2005, and Hale, Heaton, and Uglow, 2004). Better intelligence has been thought both to deter crime and to raise the chances of catching the criminals, and, in the process, reduce the need for presence on the street. The Kent Constabulary, for example, developed a variant of problem-solving to focus on burglary and motor vehicle theft. Rather than simply responding to specific incidents, the departments systematically analyzed the pattern of incidents, finding that small numbers of chronic offenders were responsible for many incidents and that patterns also include repeat victims and target locations. Based on this intelligence, Kent police began a number of strategic interventions, and the area saw a significant decline in crime. Northumbria also reported consistent annual drops in crime following its implementation of an ILP model focused on identifying chronic high-rate offenders (McGarrell, Freilich, and Chermak, 2007, p. 144; also see R. Anderson, 1997; Hale, Heaton, and Uglow, 2004; Ratcliffe, 2002, pp. 61–62).

The analytic, and more traditional, concept of ILP is rooted in the desire to improve policing practices through analysis of empirical evidence, facilitated by better and faster technologies. This movement toward evidence-based policing mirrors developments in the medical community (Sherman, 1998). Similar to evidence-based medicine, evidence-based policing recognizes that research alone is insufficient to alter practices. Another key component of ILP is the integration of the results of research into standards of policing practice. This requires the collection of data, the staffing of in-house analysts, and a mandate to integrate analysis into quality-improvement measures. These practices are in contrast to community-based policing, which does not link evidence to crime-prevention effectiveness.

The goal is "predictive policing." As it did for corporate America, the Y2K scare prompted police departments to upgrade information technology (IT) systems and become more IT-savvy. As a result, both large and small police departments—93 percent of police agencies serve fewer than 20,000 residents—have IT platforms that range from basic computer-aided dispatch and records management systems to the more-sophisticated tracking and clearing database systems utilized in major metropolitan areas. Many are now implementing or planning the transition to ILP through the use of data collection databases and various analytic tools utilized in the name of "predictive policing" (Wethal, 2009).

Britain's National Criminal Intelligence Service (NCIS) identifies the four tenets of its National Intelligence Model as targeting of offenders, management of crime and disorder hot spots, investigation of linked series of crimes and incidents, and application of preventive measures (NCIS, 2000). The drive for intelligence gathering in policing is not new in the United States. In 1971, the Law Enforcement Assistance Administration of the U.S. Department of Justice published a guide for gathering intelligence. In 1973, the National Advisory Commission on Criminal Justice Standards and Goals supported this guidance by instructing law enforcement agencies to gather and evaluate information related to policing practices (Peterson, 2005). Each state and law enforcement agency was asked to curtail organized crime and public disorder while simultaneously protecting the individual's right to privacy (National Advisory Commission, 1973, p. 250).

Beginning with the FBI's use of fingerprint collection and analysis of the reform era, the focus on evidence-based policing practices can be seen in the Kansas City experiment through CompStat during the community-policing era—all examined in a raft of scholarly studies in criminology. In fact, many tenets of CompStat, which examined the effectiveness of community-based policing, mirror the requirements of ILP. The experiment stressed four principles: timely and accurate intelligence, effective tactics, rapid deployment, and relentless follow-up and assessment (Ratcliffe, 2008). The similarities of ILP to POP have caused some confusion among scholars and practitioners alike.

ILP possesses the same focus on crime and problem-solving methodology of POP. However, the requirements of the ILP era do vary slightly. First, the data gathered by community-oriented policing and POP is statistical and incident based, while intelligence analysis examines problems on a larger scope. The Bureau of Justice Assistance specifies that "Intelligence data is the formal process of taking information and turning it into knowledge while ensuring that the information is collected, stored, and disseminated appropriately. Crime analysis data, usually collected for investigative purposes, typically does not meet the same standards . . . ." (Bureau of Justice Assistance, 2005, pp. 10–11). Second, ILP stresses the importance of analytical techniques *that are outside police officers' own judgments* to guide practices and decisions

(Osborne, 2008). This is in contrast to the inherently subjective judgments that result from personal involvement in specific communities. Where community-based policing focused on improving context-specific practices by the police themselves, ILP requires analysts that analyze data objectively.

Table 2.1 illustrates the differences between POP and ILP.

ILP utilizes a model of operations that focuses on information to direct operations, rather than the other way around. The Clients, Analysis, Partnerships, Response, and Assessment (CARPA) model, developed first by the Canadian Mounted Police, focuses on those five

Table 2.1
Differences Between Intelligence-Led Policing and Problem-Oriented Policing

Dimension	Intelligence-Led Policing	Problem-Oriented Policing
Police mission	Law enforcement	Dealing with police-relevant problems
Scope of policing	Narrowed to law enforcement	Expanded beyond law enforcement
Core drivers	Intelligence units, tasking and coordinating groups	Analysts and data
Cooperation beyond police services	Depends on enforcement	Depends on problem
Intervention focus	Person	Event pattern
Analytic inputs	Evidence and intelligence	Data
Technology	Computerized intelligence relating to cases, networks, and series	Computers and software for aggregate analysis
Preferred tactic	Arrest	Any, depends on problem
Preferred control mechanism	Incapacitation	Any, but especially blocked opportunity
Main success indicator	Serious or prolific villains caught	Police functions performed effectively
Expected benefit	Reduced crime	Reduced crime and other police-related problems

SOURCE: Tilley, 2003.

areas as the primary facets of information-driven operations. The case of the Terrorism Early Warning (TEW) group in Los Angeles, discussed in more detail in the next chapter, is a prime example of the use of this ILP model. The TEW group, a partnership of local and national law enforcement and public safety agencies, analyzed and interpreted data trends and information about events surrounding the 2000 Democratic National Convention, formulated coordinated response plans to high-probability events, and passed these plans on to their clients, the law enforcement and public safety organizations in the greater Los Angeles area. The renewed emphasis on ILP has also been reflected in the United States in such initiatives as the Global Justice Information Sharing Initiative, the Global Intelligence Working Group, and the National Criminal Intelligence Sharing Plan.

Jerry Ratcliffe, a prolific ILP scholar, describes ILP as a management philosophy or business model characterized by the following:

- **Goal:** to both achieve crime reduction and prevention and also to disrupt offender activity
- **Organization:** a top-down management approach that operates by standard guidance
- **Practices:** combination of crime analysis and criminal intelligence into crime intelligence, use of crime intelligence to objectively direct police resource decisions, focus of enforcement activities on prolific and serious offenders (Ratcliffe, 2008, p. 87).

ILP has implications for both how policing is organized and how it does its work. On the organizational side—unlike community-based policing, which gives individual police officers substantial latitude in developing their relations with local communities—ILP is necessarily more centralized. Information from different sources has to be assembled in one central place. Data collection provides the basis for the empirical analysis, and decision rules should perform as well, if not better, than the subjective judgments of individual police officers. The following quote from a senior FBI official refers to the terrorism face of ILP, but what he said applies to the crime side as well: "With this new approach, we want agents to ask if the issue that just popped into their in-box [as a conventional case] is more important than filling a critical intelligence gap. It's all about forcing them to make these tough, but important choices about how to spend your time and resources" (Rivkin and Roberto, 2007b, p. 7). In terms of daily activities, one of the key differences is that ILP entails considerable time spent identifying and handling informants, an activity that is noticeably absent from the patrol and investigation aspects of policing.

Although the development of ILP is relatively recent, there have been other examples of success. In the 1990s, the Jefferson County Sheriff's Office and the Lakewood Police Department merged vice and intelligence records and then adopted CrimNtel software to manage and share their records in 2001. In 2003, the City of Arvada Police Department also joined CrimNtel, leading to one of the greatest record-sharing efforts in the Denver area. The Rockland County Intelligence Center formed in Rockland County with similar aims in 1995. This group is governed by an oversight committee that includes the county police chiefs and municipal and county representatives and uses a multitude of databases, including the Middle Atlantic–Great Lakes Organized Crime Law Enforcement Network, the New York City Construction Authority Mobnet database, and the National Insurance Crime Bureau (Peterson, 2005).

Statistical analysis has aided in understanding and informing a variety of practices, such as racial profiling or bias in police departments around the United States. In 2002, the Cincinnati Police Department (CPD), the Fraternal Order of Police, and the American Civil Liberties Union (ACLU) agreed to improve community relations and resolve conflicts (Schell, Ridgeway, Dixon, Turner, and Riley, 2007). In 2004, RAND was commissioned to do an evaluation of these efforts over the course of five years. RAND's approach included the following:

- "a survey conducted in 2005, 2006, and 2008 of CPD officers about their perceptions of support from the community, working conditions, and other factors related to job satisfaction and performance

- a survey conducted in 2005, 2006, and 2008 of officers and citizens involved in a sample of citizen complaints against the officers and the department
- an analysis of motor-vehicle stops occurring between 2003 and 2007 for patterns of racial disparity in various aspects of the stop
- periodic observations conducted in 2005 of structured meetings between citizens and representatives of CPD
- a review of CPD statistical compilations of CPD data from 2004 to 2007
- analysis of a sample of videotaped interactions between citizens and officers during motor-vehicle stops that occurred between 2005 and 2007
- analysis of CPD staffing, recruitment, retention, and promotion patterns in 2005" (Ridgeway, Schell, Gifford, Saunders, Turner, Riley, and Dixon, 2009, p. xvi).

RAND found that community relations with the police have improved since 2005. In particular, black residents reported perceived increases in police professionalism and decreases in racial profiling, while differences in racial search rates and the length of traffic stops decreased and communication of officers during traffic stops improved. Similarly, in 2007, RAND examined the 500,000 pedestrian stops of the New York City Police Foundation made in 2006 as a part of the Stop, Question, and Frisk policy to look for signs of racial profiling (Ridgeway, Schell, Gifford, Saunders, Turner, Riley, and Dixon, 2009). The use of statistical tools found that, with a few exceptions, such as Staten Island, the New York Police Department's (NYPD's) stop-and-frisk policies did not disproportionately affect nonwhite pedestrians—a finding that was key to aiding in police-community relations.

RAND has offered similar support in other areas of policing, including the evaluation of unnecessary firearm discharges for the NYPD, which discovered characteristics that might statistically determine which officers would be involved in a shooting (Rostker, Hanser, Hix, Jensen, Morral, Ridgeway, and Schell, 2008). It should be noted, though, that while these studies have improved both policing and community attitudes toward police, they have so far stopped short of actually reducing crime, which is the key goal of these methods.

Evaluating intelligence differs from "traditional measures of law enforcement success, such as the number of arrests and indictments" achieved, which are outputs or crime rates that are measures of a near-outcome (Peterson, 2005, p. 21). All these might be thought of as "narrow" metrics. Criteria for intelligence—which might be thought of as "broad" metrics—can be developed, but doing so is more elusive than for narrow metrics. Broad metrics might include whether or not a unit has achieved more information over time, what was learned, and whether these led to shifts in investigative efforts (Bureau of Justice Assistance, 2005). Similarly, as information continues to proliferate, understanding whether or not information was shared, how widely, and with whom will be important.

Charting the Mismatch

The next chapter turns to the mismatch between the criminal threat and the way policing is organized. Police departments are organized by geography, but, increasingly, the threat is not. However, the mismatch begins internally, as the emphasis on ILP drives home. Departments typically are organized by geography, in precincts, but they also have functional divisions. Typically, the only one of those divisions that matches the geographical organization is patrolling, which is known outside the United States, variously, as "operations," "general duties," or "uniforms" (Bayley, 1992). This mismatch sets up several internal tugs of war. The functional specialists, such as detectives (criminal investigators), are by nature protective of their specialized status; they want to be distinguished from their colleagues with general duties.

So, who controls a particular operation on the ground—the geographic commander (usually a general duties officer) or the functional commander? The disputes often wind up being referred to headquarters. Most of the time the regional commanders win the tug of war, but they know from experience that seeking to get too far into the work of the specialists will only generate another appeal to headquarters.

For their part, the general-duty officers resent detectives from headquarters arriving to scoop up interesting cases (Bayley, 1992, pp. 524–525). As a result, the efforts of general officers on those crimes may become perfunctory, even though research suggests that they are in the best position to collect decisive information. In a similar way, the generalists, who typically share traffic duties with functional specialists, are likely to see that task as beneath them, not really relevant to crime-fighting, and so do it only in dangerous cases, such as drunk driving. For some forces, these tugs of war result in formal policies, ones outlining how much general-duty officers can work on particular crimes or what they can expect in assistance from specialists.

The internal fault lines particularly bear on the role of intelligence, which is central to the vision of policing set out here. Traditional law enforcement is strikingly different from classic intelligence. For example, in 1993, President George H. W. Bush was the target of a car bomb attempt during a post-presidential trip to Kuwait. The plot was foiled, and the President was never in danger. However, the Clinton administration then faced the question of how to respond: If Iraqi intelligence was responsible, was the evidence good enough to justify to the world a retaliatory strike, what our Pentagon colleagues referred to as "TLAM [Tomahawk Land Attack Missile] therapy"—that is, cruise missile strikes on Baghdad? The administration put together an unusual team of CIA intelligence officers and FBI and Justice Department law enforcement specialists.

The perspectives of the two disciplines were distinct in almost every way. Table 2.2 summarizes the differences.

For classic intelligence, the purpose is helping make better policy, and the timing is thus before the fact. The world is a blizzard of uncertainty, and so the standard is good enough to be a basis for policy. Intelligence's highest calling is protecting sources and methods, so the last thing intelligence officers want is to be in the chain of evidence or testifying in court. Traditional law enforcement is different in every way. The purpose is catching and then convicting bad guys; the point is to make cases. The timing is after the crime has been committed. The standard is high, that of a court of law, and law enforcers know that in

Table 2.2
Classic Intelligence Compared with Traditional Law Enforcement

Aspect	Intelligence	Law Enforcement
Purpose	Helping make policy	Making cases
Timing	Before the fact	After the fact
Standard	Sometimes, "good enough for government work"	Good enough for a court of law
Approach to evidence processing	Stay out of evidence chain to protect sources and methods	Must reveal some details of how they got evidence in order to convict

court they will have to reveal something of how they know what they know (Treverton, 2001b).

The interaction of the perspectives in the Bush attempt case was fascinating. If global public opinion were to be convinced, the standard had to be high, and some of the forensic methods had to be made public. However, in the end, the case seemed strong, it was presented, and Iraqi intelligence headquarters received the retaliatory strike.

Intelligence is hard to integrate on a number of grounds. Criminal behavior does not fall into neat categories, ones that match the organizations of police departments (Ratcliffe, 2007). For instance, with the exception of true lone wolves, most criminal activity is a mix of individual and group. One criminal may steal credit cards, which makes him the target of a tactical intelligence profile. But he may then engage with a group by selling the cards to a network of accomplices or by using them at establishments known to accept fraudulent credit cards.

Compounding the challenge in police departments, some departments have crime analysts but not intelligence analysis, others have the reverse, and some try to do both jobs with one set of analysts. If they do have both crime and intelligence analysts, the two groups often do not talk to one another. In any event, the two tasks are different at every level. Tactically, crime analysts mirror uniformed police officers in mapping and assessing criminal incidents, while intelligence analysts are mostly in the case-support business, helping to produce information to get convictions. At the operational level, the issue for crime analysts is mostly resource allocation: Given crime patterns, where and how should the department deploy its resources? For intelligence analysts, the operational task is understanding the nature of organized crime and gang networks. Even strategically, the two sets of analysts may have somewhat different perspectives, with the crime analyst focusing on the causes of crime, while the intelligence analyst is interested primarily in vulnerabilities in societies and how they might be exploited by organized crime (Ratcliffe, 2007, p. 18).

The result of these different approaches to analysis, plus the chance that any department may have one but not the other, is that senior leaders do not get "crime and intelligence briefings based on information that has been sufficiently analyzed and synthesized to understand the big picture" (Ratcliffe, 2007, pp. 16–17). Beneath them, crime analysis may be distributed pretty widely throughout the department but without the context that intelligence might provide, while intelligence analysis may be disseminated only in operational silos to aid the investigation and preserve the security of the case, with the result that other possible consumers, including those in the leadership, lack the richer context of criminal threats that might enable a broader approach to crime-fighting. The fusion centers, discussed in more detail below, are surely a step in the right direction, but most senior police executives still lack reliable access to information that would provide a detailed picture of crime in nearby jurisdictions.

Moreover, organizational structures are hard to change, all the more so given the culture of policing. In the words of one observer:

> Knowledge about police organization is used like a road map—once you get where you are going, you stuff it in the glove compartment. At the same time, police fight their most bitter battles over changes in organization. And politicians think abolishing or amalgamating police forces is tantamount to changing the constitution. Efforts at the reform of policing inevitably, and too often exclusively, focus on questions of location, scope, and chain of command. Proposals to assign detectives, for example, to patrol commands or to base traffic units in police stations can be as controversial as selling condoms in a convent. (Bayley, 1992, p. 510)

CHAPTER THREE

Crime Does Not Respect Jurisdiction

Crime is increasingly mismatched to the way policing is organized. Policing is still preeminently organized by geography—forces, districts, and precincts. Criminal networks, however, are not. For example, the financial institution plundered may be in Manhattan, but the cyber criminals who did the deed in Moscow, with five computer networks in between. Cooperation among police agencies has increased, but mostly in incremental ways, such as through Interpol or by jurisdictions inviting fellow officers from elsewhere to join them on "their" turf. Yet the drug gangs operating in Nogales, Sonora, are the same as those in Nogales, Arizona. The existence of different jurisdictions in the two places only offers them seams to exploit, along with some sanctuary. The U.S.-Mexico border offers vivid examples for the mismatch of jurisdictions.

More broadly, the evidence for the mismatch so far is mostly anecdotal, but the anecdotes are accumulating, and a number of these are laid out in Chapter Five. The same technologies that enable the global economy also enable global crime. Even what looks like very local crime may have distant roots or enablers. Moreover, while radically transforming jurisdictions is not yet on the agenda, developing processes to work across them does not seem to put police capacity to deal with purely local crime at risk. Rather, the communications and other technologies, with processes to match, should have a positive spillover for local crime—for instance, in warning of possible copycat crime or new criminal methods, even if the criminals involved are purely local.

For the foreseeable future, efforts to diminish the mismatch will continue to be piecemeal and ad hoc. Broader and more-formal forms of cooperation are, like Interpol, relatively weak. But less-formal bilateral or regional working arrangements are on the rise—for instance, allowing officers from other jurisdictions to pursue investigations across those jurisdictions even when the jurisdiction lines are national borders. Here, too, the fight against terror is accelerating the process and, in that sense, can have spillover benefits for policing more generally.

The Force of Jurisdictions

Examples of the mismatch are legion. Indeed, the entire system is mismatched, as the discussion of internal organization suggested. Yet, beyond internal structure, not only is policing organized by jurisdictions that match crime in fewer and fewer respects, but those jurisdictions themselves make little sense. One study of the five largest English-speaking democracies concluded that "National structures of policing reflect decisions about the geographical distribution of political power. They emerge early in national histories, and they change very little subsequently" (Bayley, 1992, p. 531). Of the five, the United States is unique in its overlapping jurisdictions, which mean that a citizen might simultaneously be policed by city, county, and state forces. As another observer put it over 70 years ago, "[T]here is . . . no such thing in the United States as a police system, not even a set of police systems within any reasonably accurate sense of the term" (B. Smith, 1940, p. 23). If the United States is unique among the five English-speaking democracies, it is not alone more generally: Italy, Spain, Belgium, and Switzerland also have overlapping jurisdictions.

The Los Angeles area is a kind of poster child for this overlap. Its 4,000 square miles contain almost 10 million people. It hosts 88 municipalities, including the City of Los Angeles. Forty-six of the municipalities have their own police department with a chief of police and usually between 40 and 150 officers at any given time. For cities like Sierra Madre or South Pasadena, which are small and relatively affluent, these departments are like small-town police departments. Other cities, like

Inglewood, Long Beach, Pasadena, and Pomona, which are bigger and are home to rich and poor alike, have substantial police departments. Long Beach, for instance, is among the 100 largest departments in the country, with detective units, task forces, and the like. These are still much smaller than the 9,900 sworn officers—that is, those who have completed police academy training—and 2,900 civilians of the Los Angeles [city] Police Department (LAPD).

The Los Angeles County Sheriff's Department (LASD) has 10,000 sworn officers and 8,000 civilians, plus 830 reserve deputies, led by an elected county sheriff. It provides jail services for the entire county, including the big cities, thus running a big medical facility, and its bailiffs serve the entire county court system—responsibilities that account for its much larger ratio of civilian to sworn officers than for LAPD. It also contracts services to 42 cities for patrol of their neighborhoods and all of their law enforcement needs. This category has grown in recent years. In the cases of Compton, Maywood, and Cudahy, the sheriff effectively took over following reports of graft and incompetence, a development that is also likely for the city of Bell. Other cities, such as Pomona, have weighed the option of turning policing over to LASD in order to save money.

Aside from the City of Los Angeles, most cities in the county defer to LASD in the investigation of major homicides and for the analysis of forensic evidence. This is true to some extent even for larger cities, such as Long Beach, Pasadena, and Pomona. Thirty-six contract for some type of specialized police service, such as search and rescue, arson and explosives, or homicide investigation; and all the county's municipalities, including the City of Los Angeles, contract for jail service.

On the whole, the relationship between the two giants, LASD and LAPD, is rivalrous but usually not acrimonious. Each regards itself as setting the standard for excellence in law enforcement. They are rivals in competing for the best new recruits, but that is a good thing. They are not rivals in taking on gang crime. One potential source of friction is overcrowding in the prisons that the Sheriff's Office manages for the entire county, including LAPD. Any threat to release prisoners to alleviate overcrowding or budget problems would rankle LAPD the most because the City of Los Angeles accounts for such a large portion of the crime and criminal population in the county.

Beyond the two big forces, however, cooperation is mostly operational and ad hoc, not systematic and proactive. Santa Monica, for instance, is surrounded by Los Angeles. Yet the two do not routinely share information about either homeland security or other threats. As one observer put it, "[T]he Santa Monica Police Department conducts policing duties, for the most part, independent of and without concern for the needs of the Los Angeles Police Department and vice versa" (Sanchez, 2009, pp. 1–2). Sharing is all the more hindered because many departments do not have the technical platforms—data and voice networks—to make that sharing easy. As late as 2009, Santa Monica, for instance, had different networks than Culver City, five miles away (which is also surrounded by Los Angeles), so the two could not easily communicate.

When cooperation is more formal, it usually is regional, organized around a common crime threat, and in the form of a task force. The LA Intra-Agency Metropolitan Police Apprehension Crime Task Force (LA Impact) is an example. It was formed in 1991, bringing together local, state, and federal law enforcement agencies across the county:

> In the late 1990s, public opinion polls showed that Southern Californians believed narcotics to be the most serious criminal problem faced by law enforcement. Because of the crackdown of drugs entering through Miami, drug smugglers had shifted their activities to the west, and many law enforcement agencies considered Los Angeles County to be the new drug distribution hub for the entire nation. (Pasadena Police Department, 2011)

Drug trafficking continues to be the mission of LA Impact.

Not surprisingly, what is true in one metropolitan area is true in spades across the country. On September 11, 2001, New York City's police and fire departments could not easily talk to one another. The problem, one highlighted by the 9/11 commission, was notable again in the response to Hurricane Katrina in 2005. Yet, despite those failures and despite some $7 billion in federal grants and other spending, a single nationwide public safety radio system is still years away (Wyatt,

2010). In one sense, now is the right moment to embrace this element of a vision of the future, for the focus is now on "the next generation of emergency communications, wireless broadband" (Wyatt, 2010). The challenge in working toward that vision of the future is to make it succeed where previous attempts have failed.

Yet, it, too, is bedeviled by the same impediments on display since 9/11, as well as some new ones. In mid-2010, the U.S. Department of Commerce gave $220 million to five regional efforts to build some of the first wireless broadband public safety networks (Wyatt, 2010). These efforts would do just what the future of policing requires. One program would let San Francisco, Oakland, and other jurisdictions in the Bay area talk, transfer files, and share videos, and another would do the same for Los Angeles Country. In Los Angeles, the initiative, dubbed LA-SafetyNet, aimed to connect 34,000 first responders across the county's different police, fire, and public health jurisdictions. It would

> construct 176 new wireless sites and leverage 114 existing sites to serve greater Los Angeles and provide broadband access, equipment, and service to community anchor institutions across the region . . . [and] . . . serve as a demonstration project for national implementation of 700 MHz interoperable public safety wireless broadband networks. (Mayor of the City of Los Angeles, 2010)

It would be managed by the Los Angeles Regional Interoperable Communications System, created in 2009, and overseen by a 17-member board of stakeholders (Mayor of the City of Los Angeles, 2010).

Yet, these initial efforts are being constructed before there is any broad agreement on standards for equipment and networks. As a result, there is no guarantee that other jurisdictions that seek to join the networks in the future will be operating, literally, on the same wavelength (Wyatt, 2010). Beyond standards, there is a debate over control. Public safety advocates would like to control the spectrum over which the new network operates. In particular, the conversion of television stations from analog to digital freed up space on the spectrum. Congress set aside a 10-megahertz (10-MHz) band for a public safety wireless network, as part of a 24-MHz allocation, and also instructed the Federal

Communications Commission (FCC) to auction off another 10-MHz band that would include a network built to public safety specifications. When the auction was held, in 2008, it failed to attract the minimum bid (Wyatt, 2010). Now public safety advocates say that they need all 34 MHz to build a dedicated public safety network.

For the FCC, though, that would be like building separate highways for police, fire departments, and other public safety agencies. It would be better, the FCC argues, to liken the spectrum to current highways: Routinely, public safety and other uses would occur together, with public safety preempting if need be—the cyber equivalent of ordinary cars pulling off the highway so fire engines can pass. Yet, elected officials find it hard to say no to fire and police departments, and the concern is thus growing that the debate will drag on while the window for wireless broadband closes. In particular, the broader debate might overshadow progress made in linking voice systems, which will for a long time be the dominant form of public safety communications (Wyatt, 2010). Indeed, as the chief of the FCC's public safety and homeland security bureau put it to Congress in 2010, "There is nothing that is inevitable about having a nationwide interoperable system. . . . [T]he last 75 years of public safety communications teaches us that there are no natural or market forces" to make it happen (Barnett, 2010).

Lest this challenge of working across jurisdictions should seem a purely U.S. pathology, in Canada about 70 percent of officers are sworn in under local, municipal, or regional jurisdictions, which means that they cannot operate as police officers outside their geographical designation. The two exceptions that have been acknowledged by lower courts include hot pursuit and the existence of a "sufficient nexus" between the two jurisdictions. Both of those exceptions are short term. To get around this and allow for extra-provincial travel and assistance, officers must be sworn in as "special constables" in the province they are going to operate in, as well as all those in between their home jurisdiction and the one they will operate in—between their home and away fields, so to speak (Schumacher, 2003).

Sharing information is difficult not just because of the impediments that are built into the culture of police organizations or the desire of political jurisdictions to have their "own" police, but, in the United States, they are also built into the culture itself (Reiss, 1992). Given the large number of small departments, even in a big metropolitan area like Los Angeles, it would be unsurprising if there were moves to consolidate departments in the interests both of effectiveness against crime and efficiency in cost. Such movements do arise, but relatively rarely. When consolidation occurs, it usually takes one of two forms. The first is consolidating separate forces into a metropolitan police department when a metropolitan county form of government is adopted. Davidson County (Nashville), Tennessee, is an example.

The other form of consolidation is contract policing. Small departments contract with a county sheriff's department or a large municipality to provide police service. Sometimes, this change is the result of failure, as it has been in Los Angeles: Small jurisdictions run into serious financial trouble or mounting corruption that forces the department into what is, in effect, receivership. Other times, it occurs simply to save money. California law facilitates contract policing. Yet, for all the contracting and consolidation, there has never been pressure for a real national police force, similar to those in Britain or Canada— one much bigger than the 13,000-plus special agents of the FBI and with broader authority. Indeed, the idea seems anathema to Americans. Instead, the current patchwork quilt of organizations seems to fit with American ideals of decentralized power, authority, and decisionmaking. In these circumstances, it is less surprising that there is little formal integration of police departments or that most cooperation is operational, case by case. Formal arrangements hardly extend beyond the contracting out of policing or state-supervised minimum standards for policing or mandated training.

Trying to Do Better: More-Formal Cooperation

These traditions of operating independently, plus the technical challenges of diverse platforms, also afflict more-explicit initiatives in sharing across regions or states. September 11 added impetus to such sharing, but the need was recognized well before those attacks. Los Angeles

County pioneered with the TEW group, which began in the mid-1990s (Sullivan, 2001, p. 124). It was explicitly designed to anticipate emerging threats, especially terrorism, and to try to deny networked adversaries the advantage of working in the seams of existing policing organizations. It sought to blend networking with traditional organization by including law enforcement, fire service, and health authorities at all levels of government. It aimed at bottom-up sharing but strove to be anticipatory and not just to respond to operational needs. It came to include interested and expert nongovernmental members and was, in general, an open forum. In addition to its plenary open forum, it had three subcommittees—a Playbook Committee for developing response information (target) folders and playbooks to guide response, an Emerging Threat Committee to assess threats over the next five to ten years, and a Net Assessment Group to support decisions in actual threats or attacks (Sullivan, 2001). The TEW model was reproduced in different forms in a number of places around the United States.

This model is worth pausing over because it represented a bottom-up but systematic approach to working around the fault lines of jurisdiction. Two episodes illustrate its working style and effect. TEW was designed to link "real time information with strategy and emergency response" (Grossman, 2005, p. 30). One of the essential components of this overall capability was the ability to synthesize large amounts of information across time and space to identify key patterns and precursors of a valid threat and then disseminate actionable intelligence on how to recognize and respond to such a threat; within TEW, this process was referred to as Indications and Warning (I&W).

Shortly after its formation, TEW's I&W capability was tested. In late 1998, Southern California experienced over 40 anthrax threats, all of which were hoaxes (Iden, 2002). Many cities were taken by surprise, but TEW had made Los Angeles ready. Gathering information from a variety of sources—most public, some classified—TEW was aware by August 1998 of the spread of hoax threats across the country, plainly raising the potential for copycat events in Los Angeles. TEW monthly meetings raised the issue of developing plans to deal with potential anthrax threats in Los Angeles (Grossman, 2005). By November, it was decided to formulate policies for dealing with threats, and an advisory with these guidelines was disseminated for all field units of TEW member agencies by mid-December (The Advisory Panel to Assess Domestic Response Capabilities for Terrorism Involving Weapons of Mass Destruction [Gilmore Commission], 2000, p. G-12). Because of the I&W processes of TEW, policies were already in place before an anthrax hoax arrived in Los Angeles.

Additionally, TEW went further to capture and codify informal knowledge on the part of first responders when anthrax hoaxes finally did appear. The first rash of anthrax hoax threats arrived in Los Angeles in mid-December, with seven threats in just ten days, the first several costing Angelenos well over half a million dollars each until responders learned to recognize the hoaxes and adjust the response downward (The Advisory Panel to Assess Domestic Response Capabilities for Terrorism Involving Weapons of Mass Destruction [Gilmore Commission], 2000). After the first wave, representatives of TEW member agencies met to institutionalize the knowledge their first responders had acquired in discriminating between real threats and hoaxes for use in future incidents. Member agency representatives met and developed "a structured set of indicators that provided the means to assess the need to respond, or not" (Grossman, 2005, p. 44). These indicators were disseminated to all field units within days of their development and were immediately used in subsequent responses to calls concerning possible anthrax contamination (The Advisory Panel to Assess Domestic Response Capabilities for Terrorism Involving Weapons of Mass Destruction [Gilmore Commission], 2000). Using these indicators helped responders properly assess the validity of the threat, conserving scarce time and resources, as well as saving tens or hundreds of people the inconvenience of unnecessary decontamination.

A second example tested TEW's ability as an organization to respond to threats, both real and potential. This was the 2000 Democratic National Convention, held in Los Angeles in August of that year. Not surprisingly, given the convention as a focal point, thousands of protesters announced their intention to demonstrate during the convention. The presence of the President, as well as members of Congress and high-profile political figures, in a charged, target-rich environment with lots of media coverage created a situation ripe for potential disaster. Recognizing this fact, TEW worked to compile information on the tactics, techniques, and procedures (TTPs) used by the protesting groups in order for police, fire, and health organizations to better anticipate and respond to (or altogether avoid) problems arising from the clash of protesters, politicians, and police. While the U.S. Secret Service was busy coordinating the actions and operations of law enforcement and public safety organizations necessary for the convention, TEW was "observing and evaluating the bigger picture to identify trends, potentials and indicators of what, where, and how acts of disruption might occur" (Grossman, 2005, p. 46).

TEW pulled information from other law enforcement agencies, public source materials, and units in the field to provide people on the ground with relevant information. For example, a field unit reported that piles of rocks were apparently intentionally stacked in a protest area. Coupled with the prior information that TEW had gathered about the TTPs of the protesting group, TEW surmised that the protesters were intending to use the rocks against police during their demonstrations. It put out an advisory to this effect, and the protesters were disarmed (Grossman, 2005).

This example, especially, strikes home the value of having an organization tasked with gathering and examining all the relevant information as a whole. Each piece of information alone, either about the group's tactics or the presence of the rocks, might not have been enough to warrant a response on the part of law enforcement until protesters were already throwing rocks at police officers and the story was on its way to front pages across the country. Yet, with the complete picture, law enforcement was able to disarm the group without incident while still preserving the integrity of the political process (Grossman, 2005).

However, in Los Angeles but also elsewhere, TEW groups were largely superseded after September 11 by fusion centers, an initiative sponsored by the Department of Homeland Security (DHS). By the end of 2009, there were 74 fusion centers around the country. The 9/11 Commission diagnosis included weak sharing of information across the federal, state, and local levels as a contributor to the disaster, and the fusion centers were, in part, a response. They "built to some degree upon interagency relationships that preceded the post-9/11 focus on counterterrorism" (Willis, Lester, and Treverton, 2009, p. 353). Long before the fusion center initiative, in 1967, the National Crime Information Center (NCIC) was created as a repository of crime data from across the country. Housed within the FBI, the system was designed to be shared between the FBI and state and local agencies. Information fed to it from criminal justice agencies at all levels, as well as from foreign agencies and authorized courts, is accessible to federal, state, and local law enforcement 24 hours a day, seven days a week. Yet, it is dependent on what is reported to it (NCIC, undated).

Anticipating the next chapter's focus on the role of emerging technology, Virginia became dissatisfied with the one-way flow of information. Each Virginia police jurisdiction produced a monthly report summarizing crime data that was sent to the state police and then on to the FBI, but the one-way chain did not lend itself to cooperative regional analysis and tracking. To address this shortcoming, engineers at Virginia Tech University developed a web-based search tool (the Web-Based Crime Analysis Toolkit) to enable officers across jurisdictions to query crimes using various input data to generate graphs, reports, and crime-mapping trends (Ast, Mines, Mukhopadhyay, Brown, and Conklin, 2007).

Similar to the older FBI-sponsored Joint Terrorism Task Forces (JTTFs),

> fusion centers co-locate analysts from several agencies in order to facilitate the integration of several streams of information. . . . The responsibility of the centers is to fuse foreign intelligence with domestic information in order to facilitate improved decision-making on issues of counterterrorism, crime, and emergency response.[1] Their membership is determined by local and regional need and security priorities. Although they are state-created and -based law enforcement entities, most fusion centers are partially funded by DHS [which has also seconded intelligence analysts to them]. (Willis, Lester, and Treverton, 2009, p. 353)

---

[1] This and the next paragraph also draw on Masse, O'Neil, and Rollins, 2007.

The article continues (Willis, Lester, and Treverton, 2009, p. 354):

> The fusion centers are intended to complement the JTTFs. If JTTFs work on cases once identified, the fusion centers are meant to assemble *strategic intelligence* at the regional level and pass the appropriate information on to the investigators in the task forces. In practice, the fusion centers are very much a work in progress, one displaying all the challenges of jurisdiction. Their missions vary based on regional requirements and resources. Organizationally, they differ considerably from one another in terms of organization, management, personnel and participation. Communications between centers ranges from problematic to non-existent. The centers' access to technology and intelligence information is uneven. Not all fusion centers even have state-wide intelligence systems. According to the Congressional Research Service, "The flow of information from the private sector to fusion centers is largely sporadic, event driven, and manually facilitated" (Masse, O'Neil, and Rollins, 2007, p. 29). They also do not all have access to law enforcement data. The problem of diverse platforms that was widely criticized immediately after the September 11 attacks still exists. Security clearances remain a bar to sharing, though the situation is improving. In 2007, roughly half the staff of the average fusion center (totaling about 27) had Secret clearances, about 6 had Top Secret and one had [a] Secret Compartmented Intelligence (SCI) [clearance].

As for the JTTFs before them, the obstacles the fusion centers run into in getting local officers cleared can be as much personal as procedural: More than one crusty local officer has said to a young FBI agent, with more or less scorn in his voice, "*You're* going to clear *me?*" (Stewart and Morris, 2009, p. 294.) In addition, "[b]ecause of the huge number of information systems and the resulting duplication, analysts are inundated with floods of information of variable quality" (Willis, Lester, and Treverton, 2009, p. 354). As a review of the Los Angeles fusion center, called the Joint Regional Intelligence Center (JRIC), put it,

[A]n overbroad intelligence report distributed by the LA JRIC . . . offers no perceived value for police agencies and is not frequently used to deploy police resources. Typically, the LA JRIC collects and distributes open source material or newsworthy articles in an effort to inform their clients. As a result local independent chiefs feel they cannot use the intelligence to increase operational capacity or deploy police resources to combat crime or terrorism. (Sanchez, 2009, pp. 3–4)

In addition (Willis, Lester, and Treverton, 2009, p. 354),

although much rhetoric is expended on the importance of a cyclical information flow between the fusion centers and the federal intelligence community, the information cycle tends to be rather one-directional. From the perspective of the fusion centers themselves, the value of information becomes opaque once sent to the federal intelligence agencies. This lack of a feedback loop creates both resentment and inefficiency in the relationship between federal entities and the fusion centers.

Things have improved from the days when local authorities reported that, if they called the FBI, they never received a call back, but there is a long way to go. In the counterterrorism realm, in particular, it is not clear in many jurisdictions how or if tips from state and local authorities that are not deemed to rise to the level of JTTF cases get registered in the system.

Willis, Lester, and Treverton (2009, p. 355) also add that

there has been lingering concern about issues of civil liberties and fusion centers, mainly because of public perception of lack of transparency in their operations. A range of reports, including one published by the ACLU in December 2007, brought up concerns that the expansion of intelligence gathering and sharing in these centers threatens the privacy of Americans (German and Stanley, 2007). Some of the concerns raised by the ACLU stem from the wide range of participants involved in the fusion centers, including the private sector and the military. The report argues that breaking down the many barriers between [the] public and private sector[s]; intelligence and law enforcement; and military and civil institutions could lead to abuses of private and other civil liberties, particularly if a strong and clear legal framework isn't established to guide operations within the centers.

These concerns nicely foreshadow concerns that will arise over the vision of future policing set out in this book.

The fusion centers are likely to take a variety of paths in the future. Virtually all are moving away from a singular focus on terrorism to an all-crimes, or even all-hazards, approach—probably a happy spillover from the preoccupation with terrorism to broader policing. In some places, such as Iowa, where terrorism is a minor threat, the center is explicitly in the business of driving ILP. Other centers will simply fade away if and as federal support diminishes and contributing public safety agencies decide that their personnel are more valuable "at home," rather than seconded to a fusion center.

Policing Across Borders: The United States and Mexico

If working across one metropolitan area is hard enough, imagine the challenges of policing across borders, both internal and, especially, external. Here, too, the examples are legion but nowhere more visibly on display than at the U.S.-Mexico border. The importance of Mexico to the United States hardly has to be underscored. It is the United States' second-largest trading partner, third-largest source of oil, and largest source of immigrants (Treverton, 2009, p. 55). Mexico is hardly "a failed state in the sense of Somalia, but it has failed in two critical senses [the first crucial to this discussion]—legitimate authorities long ago lost both their monopoly over the use of force and their fiscal effectiveness, that is, their capacity to tax citizens enough so the state can function. . . . [T]he security situation in Northern Mexico deteriorated so precipitously that the government of President Felipe Calderón" committed more than 50,000 military troops to the drug war in the four years after taking office in December 2006, plus an estimated 30,000 federal police officers (Treverton, 2010, p. 34). The United

States provided $1.5 billion in assistance through Plan Mérida, mostly military and technological in nature.[2] The military and police, however, distrust each other and resist operating together. American officials seemed to have lost confidence in the Mexican army and turned increasingly to the navy and its small special forces, which killed drug lord Arturo Beltran Leyva in a luxurious Cuernavaca apartment in December 2009—apparently after the army refused to act on U.S.-provided intelligence (Wilkinson and Ellingwood, 2010).

Yet, border violence has escalated, with some 34,000 killed since late 2006. (Figure 3.1 shows the mushrooming of clearly drug-related killing.) The difference between 2007 and 2008 is particularly striking (Gonzalbo, 2011). That turned around more than a decade of declining homicide rates nationwide. Even during those years of decline, the violence was concentrated in a few states, a situation that sharpened after the increase. Not only was the violence concentrated in a hand-

Figure 3.1
Drug-Related Killing in Mexico, 2007–2010

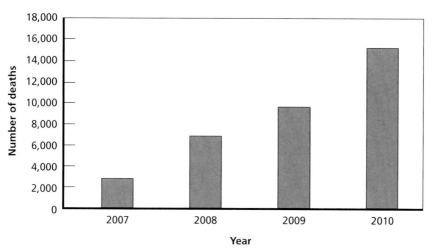

SOURCE: Mexican government statistics, compiled at "Mexico Drug War Murders," undated.
RAND *MG1102-3.1*

---

[2]   The White House fact sheet on the initiative, which also includes Central America, is available at U.S. Department of State, 2009.

ful of states—Baja California, Chihuahua, Durango, Guerrero, and Sinaloa—but within those states it was concentrated in a few urban areas. Tijuana, for instance, accounted for half of Baja California's population but almost three-quarters of its homicides in 2008–2009. More ominously, while the first deployments of the Mexican military, in December 2006, were followed the next year by declining homicide rates in several states, like Michoacán, the rates exploded in 2008 in the five most violent states, where the military was also deployed. As suggested earlier, the connection between policing inputs, in this case the deployment of the military, and outputs or near outcomes, like the homicide rate, is tricky because so many other factors are at play. However, at a minimum, the statistics do not support the argument that the anticrime strategy of deploying the military was working, at least not in the short run.

A weekend of violence in March 2010 "took the lives of dozens of Mexicans and, for the first time, of Americans connected to the U.S. Consulate in Ciudad Juárez" (Woodrow Wilson International Center for Scholars, 2010). At the end of January 2010 in Ciudad Juárez, "fifteen people were killed and twelve wounded as they celebrated a sports event at home" (Woodrow Wilson International Center for Scholars, 2010). The violence has increased even in places, such as Tijuana, where the government at some points seemed to be "winning." In September 2010, after one of its photographers was killed by gunmen, the Juárez newspaper *El Diario de Juárez* published a long editorial asking the drug cartels explicitly, "What do you want from us?" ("Qué Quieren de Nosotros?" 2010). The editorial sought a truce with the cartel, one that would end violence and stop the attacks against the media in Mexico. It asked directly, "What is it that you want from us, what is it that you want us to publish or refrain from publishing, so that we can know what to expect."

Superficially, the border seems to be working. The cross-border spillover of violence is a particular concern, but it is one that should not be exaggerated—at least not yet: El Paso, just across the river from Ciudad Juárez, is among the least violent cities in the United States, with about 20 murders in 2009, a rate of about three per 100,000. The rate in Ciudad Juárez was over 170 per 100,000 during the same period

(Olson, 2010). Still, recent events have sharpened the sense that, just as there is no military solution to the violence, so too are the border and fence no solution. An indirect piece of evidence is the suspension of expansion of the "virtual" wall, announced by the U.S. Department of Homeland Security in March 2010 (Archibold, 2010) and then stopped altogether in 2011. Over the long term, Mexico and the border will be increasing focal points for U.S. security policy, while the lack of success and the perceived collateral damage of a quasi-military approach will spur increased interest in other approaches, ranging from an emphasis on social programs in the hardest-hit Mexican cities to some accommodation with the traffickers to some decriminalization of drugs (Dresser, undated).

Arms smuggling is, to some extent, the mirror image of drug trafficking, for while narcotics use has increased domestically in Mexico, the State Department's *2007 International Narcotics Control Strategy Report* (U.S. Department of State, 2007) estimated that about 90 percent of the cocaine that enters the United States is trafficked through Mexico. Arms flow in the other direction, though exactly how many is unclear (Treverton, 2010, p. 34). American politicians and officials of the U.S. Bureau of Alcohol, Tobacco, Firearms and Explosives have used the number 90 percent, but that turns out to be the percentage of weapons submitted to the United States by Mexico and successfully traced—perhaps a fifth or a sixth of the weapons found at Mexican crime scenes. In any event, the weapons are more and more sophisticated. Where police used to find *cuernos de chivo*—goat's horns, Mexican slang for AK-47s—they now find grenades and rockets. Moreover, the traffickers are enlisting the protection of special operations forces, such as the Kaibiles (former Guatemalan special operations forces) and the Zetas, those one-time enforcers for, and then opponents of, the Gulf Cartel who may have been involved in the killing of David Hartley (Treverton, 2010, pp. 34–35).

It is plain that the problems cannot be fenced out. They are already here. According to the *National Drug Threat Assessment 2010*, of about 20 gangs with significant influence on the U.S. drug market, all but two had affiliations with some Mexican drug-trafficking organization, and about a dozen of the gangs were affiliated with more than one (National Drug Intelligence Center, 2010). In addition (Treverton, 2010, p. 35),

> [t]he migrants are here, and the great majority of new ones indicate that they intend to make the United States their permanent home. Perversely, tighter control of the borders discourages back-and-forth flow, and so encourages migrants to stay longer (Cornelius, 2006). It has also been a boon to people-smugglers (coyotes). Although the Bush administration approach to Mexican migration was stillborn, it at least proved that a middle ground, combining some measure of temporary work programs with a path to legalizing the status of the undocumented, might be possible.

In the long run, there is no alternative to somehow altering jurisdictions in two ways—first, incorporating local law enforcement and antigang community development across the four U.S. border states and their Mexican counterparts, and, second, recognizing that the problem is no longer confined to the border but now reaches to Guatemala and other parts of the hemisphere. Both would reflect "community" policing, with a very extended definition of community. For all the reasons set out in the next section, however, that cooperation probably will have to be relatively informal for the foreseeable future. It will link police and intelligence authorities from not just the United States and Mexico but other countries as well.

The problem areas are twofold. First, American officials, both federal and state, have little confidence in their Mexican counterparts, regarding them as inefficient, corrupt, or both. That fact has bedeviled the U.S.-Mexican security and policing partnership since the beginning. The second is that, at various points in advancing cooperation, there will be thresholds that visibly blur jurisdictions, like permitting U.S. authorities to operate in certain ways in Mexico, with and perhaps without Mexican counterparts. Those will become political issues. Part of the reason for the Mexican army's uneven cooperation with the United States is the shadow of history in its conception of itself as the nation's guardian against an expansionist United States.

The Limits of International Cooperation

The traditional model of international police cooperation was focused on short-term collaboration to solve a single case or catch a single criminal who had crossed jurisdictional boundaries. Cooperation across jurisdictions usually took the form of bilateral liaison rather than more-integrated cooperation. Yet, as transnational organized criminal and gang networks evolve to operate permanently within several jurisdictions, so, too, has there been a move to build sustained security-intelligence networks. This trend has been dubbed "global metropolitan policing" because it involves both horizontal and vertical networks to integrate local-level metropolitan police with national law enforcement and intelligence organizations, private organizations, and intelligence, as well as with other local metropolitan forces abroad (Sullivan and Wirtz, 2009).

The terrorist threat, in particular, has driven formal information-sharing and collaboration agreements horizontally across jurisdictions. The NYPD is in a class by itself, having placed liaison officers in law enforcement agencies in many corners of the globe—not always to the delight of such U.S. federal agencies as DHS or the FBI (Sullivan and Wirtz, 2009). These agreements outline mechanisms for cooperation, as well as ways to protect the rule of law when outside officers step in. In addition, as local departments improve their ability to cooperate across jurisdictions, there will be less need for vertical liaison bodies to act as coordinators or go-betweens for the cooperating departments. This form of collaboration is very much a work in progress. And in the end, it, too, will depend on local enforcement officers, whose job it will be to become better integrated into the community they serve. "The law enforcement response to . . . transnational threats posed by organized crime and 3rd-generation gangs must build practices related to community interaction, investigation, intelligence, and enforcement" (Sullivan and Wirtz, 2009, p. 5).

So far, given the constraints of jurisdiction, it is no surprise that international efforts at cooperation, especially relatively formal ones, have been weak. Surely, there is no lack of initiatives at cooperation. For instance, the International Association of Chiefs of Police (IACP) is the world's oldest and largest nonprofit membership organization of police executives, with over 20,000 members in over 89 different countries. IACP's leadership consists of the operating chief executives of international, federal, state, and local agencies of all sizes (IACP, 2011). In September 2009, the IACP hosted its first-ever global policing summit, which focused on the threat of increasing youth recruitment by terrorist organizations.

Like intelligence services, police departments sometimes find it easier to cooperate with fellow police departments than with other agencies of their own government. Yet, that cooperation, internationally, is best done beneath the radar of high politics, and formal institutions almost necessarily require the blessing, if not the involvement, of national politicians. In the view of one observer, police can cooperate with other police precisely because they are similar bureaucratic organizations. Yet, on this argument, that cooperation can take place only if they achieve relative autonomy from their political centers. If they do not, international cooperation will remain limited, mostly confined to states that are politically akin either in ideology or through alliance or other long association (Deflem, 2000, p. 744). The good news is that, while autonomy is affected by many political currents, internal organization is mostly the result of police tradition and practice. The latter may be hard to change but at least implies that as nations grow richer, their police forces will converge in organization (Bayley, 1992, p. 531).

Yet, while police departments may by relatively similar in structure and organization, this is not to say that there are not serious differences in capabilities, willingness, and political and social contexts—in particular, cooperation across jurisdictions with differing levels of equipment, manpower, professionalism, or political support. The U.S.-Mexico border is a case in point (Deflem, 2004). The concern on the American side about corruption in the Mexican force has already been mentioned in this chapter, and there is also a splitting of duties and responsibilities among departments on both sides. Given the disparity in size, the resulting relationship between U.S. and Mexican forces tends toward one of dependence and inequality.

Just as is true of cooperation across jurisdictions within the United States, most of the international cooperation is operational, police force with police force, driven by particular cases. For instance, in 2010, an Eastern European criminal hacker group cracked the encryption code on the Atlanta-based branch of the Royal Bank of Scotland and extracted about $9.4 million within less than four days. However, law enforcement in Estonia worked with the FBI and the U.S. Secret Service to bring the ringleader in for justice. That same year, the FBI, along with Spanish and Slovenian law enforcement, managed to arrest "three suspected operators of the Mariposa botnet, a collection of infected computers used to steal passwords, credit card data, and bank account information worldwide" (Clayton, 2010).

Sometimes, international cooperation can take the form of a "coalition of the willing," all the more so if the willing states are friends. Operation Green Ice in the early 1990s, targeting the Cali drug cartel, is a case in point. In 1989, the U.S. Drug Enforcement Administration (DEA) created its own bank, Trans America Ventures Associates (TARA), to establish its bona fides in the financial community. The ruse was so convincing that

> *Hispanic Business Weekly* listed TARA as one of the top 500 Hispanic Corporations in America. Undercover agents then posed as money launderers and offered to pick up funds anywhere in the world. . . . During the course of the investigation, DEA agents laundered more than $20 million for the Colombia-based cartels. . . . [C]artel operatives asked the undercover agents to provide money laundering services in Europe, Canada, and the Caribbean. Consequently, Operation Green Ice was expanded into a coordinated international law enforcement effort involving Canada, the Cayman Islands, Colombia, Costa Rica, Italy, Spain, the United Kingdom, and the United States.
>
> In September 1992, undercover agents finally arranged a meeting with top-ranking Cali financial managers at locations in the United States, Italy, Spain, and Costa Rica. The drug lords arrived, expecting to discuss plans for their criminal business, but instead were arrested. . . . Operation Green Ice led to the arrest of seven of the Cali mafia's top financial managers, the seizure of more than $50 million in assets worldwide, and the arrest of 177

persons, including 44 in the United States. (U.S. Drug Enforcement Administration, undated)

The operation also created its own heroine, Heidi Landgraf, a rookie DEA agent who, beginning in 1990, went undercover for two years as a money launderer in the agency's most successful sting operation, targeting the Cali drug cartel in Colombia and the Sicilian Mafia in Italy (Investigation Discovery, 2011).

The U.S. Treasury's Financial Crimes Enforcement Network (FINCEN) is another example of building international cooperation by operation and example (P. Williams, 2001, pp. 96–97). It combats money laundering "by making it more difficult to introduce dirty money into the financial system without triggering either cash transaction reports (CTRs) or suspicious activity reports (SARs)" (P. Williams, 2001, p. 96). It was created to address drug trafficking and got a boost in the fight against terror. It is a model of what has become known as a financial intelligence unit (FIU). Other countries have emulated FINCEN. Australia, for example, has its Transaction Reports and Analysis Center, known as AUSTRAC, while in Bermuda there is also a financial investigation unit (P. Williams, 2001, p. 96).

A group of FIUs came together well before 9/11, in 1995, as the Egmont Group to meet regularly in plenary while exchanging information through a secure website. As of mid-2010, the Egmont Group had 120 operating units in as many countries, more than double its membership in 2000. "Although the national FIUs vary considerably in terms of skills, resources, and available technology, the network facilitates a multinational effort to combat money laundering" (P. Williams, 2001, p. 97).

Events since 9/11 have been a test of international cooperation. While those events spurred international cooperation in counterterrorism both in principle and in fact, police cooperation across nations has not always been apparent, particularly when international institutions, such as Interpol, are involved and when cases are politically sensitive (Deflem and Maybin, 2005). One example was a former Chechen government representative, Akhmed Zakayev, charged with terrorism through Interpol. According to an analysis of counterterrorism strategies at Interpol, he was charged

> [at the] request of Russian authorities. He was freed by Danish authorities in early December 2002 because no evidence was found against him and soon thereafter was released on bail from a London prison. Another instance of lack of cooperation at the international level by police agencies, despite their formal participation in Interpol, is the case of former Peruvian president Alberto Fujimori. An Interpol notice for Fujimori, who is now living in self-exile in Japan, was placed by Peruvian authorities in 2001. But Japanese police and justice authorities have not sought extradition for Fujimori because he has, in the meantime, become a Japanese citizen. (Deflem and Maybin, 2005)

On the other hand, the FBI regarded Interpol's Operation International Fugitive Roundup and Arrest (known as Operation Infra-Red) as a focused effort to apprehend fugitives by promoting the timely exchange of information among the organization's member countries and by soliciting the help of the public worldwide (FBI, 2010). Launched in May 2010,

> the operation targeted 450 convicted or wanted persons whose names were submitted by 29 participating countries. In early July [2010], Interpol issued a call for public assistance to locate these individuals. Since that time, 114 fugitives have been located or arrested, and new information on 323 of the cases has been provided—including possible locations, photographs, and telephone numbers.

> To assist with Operation Infra-Red, the Bureau assigned several agents and other personnel to Interpol headquarters in Lyon, France, and is offering additional support from . . . [the] Violent Crimes/Major Offenders Unit and Directorate of Intelligence at FBI Headquarters in Washington. (FBI, 2010)

The FBI's willingness to cooperate was spurred by the fact that some on the Interpol list were on the FBI's ten most wanted list as well.

Europe is an intriguing example of the barriers to and the possibilities of working across jurisdictions. There is no unified place called "Europe." Rather, Europe has over a million police officers whose structures, roles, and rules are just some of the differentiating characteristics. In centralized systems, such as Denmark, Finland, and Ireland, one police service is headed by a lone chief. By contrast, in Britain—a unitary, not federal, state—there are still 50 separate police forces. The role of prosecutors in a member nation can affect the varying level of investigation a police officer has and whether the focus of the police is on evidence-gathering after the fact or preventive measures. In Britain, phone taps cannot be used as evidence in court, but closed-circuit TV footage can be. In contrast, France is the reverse: Phone taps are considered compliant with civil liberties, but closed-circuit TV footage raises issues of intrusiveness. The European Union (EU) has no power to structure police forces for member states, so it has been working to develop common standards and practices to address crime that crosses borders, especially crimes involving drugs, organized crime, and human trafficking.

Areas of cooperation include Schengen (border-free) countries, in which police forces are allowed to pursue crimes across borders without prior notification. To complement this "hot pursuit" policy, officers in the Schengen area have access to a multinational police database (Schengen Information System) that tracks suspects, stolen goods, and cars (Brady, 2007). Frontex is the EU external border agency created in 2005 to coordinate efforts among member nations to combat illegal immigration in the Atlantic and Mediterranean coastal areas. Following an April 2007 agreement to establish rapid border intervention deployment units, the EU home affairs commissioner, Franco Frattini, described the agency as "the best ever example of European solidarity" (Goldirova, 2007). Twenty-seven nations comprising 450 national experts contribute to this body, which can require member states whose borders are under "urgent and exceptional" strain of illegal migration to deploy units on as little notice as five working days. Permanent coastal patrols were set in place in 2007 to monitor flashpoint areas of illegal entry. Frontex has at its disposal a fleet of 20 airplanes, 30 helicopters, and over 100 vessels to help in its mission.

Bilateral and multilateral agreements between countries also enhance cooperation. For instance, in preparation for the 2006 World Cup, a treaty between Germany and Austria allowed police forces to operate under each other's command as needed to enable undercover operations in the other's respective territory. EU police chiefs collaborate through the European Police Chiefs' Task Force (PCTF), which meets regularly to exchange information, as well as to plan and operate joint investigations. The European PCTF organizes its work using multicountry policing teams that are divided per investigation, with one country—typically the one most affected by the investigation—acting as the team "driver." The system is known as Comprehensive Operational Strategic Planning for the Police (COSPOL), and it was instrumental in a May 2005 operation to crack down on child pornographers. Swedish-led, the team comprised hundreds of officers representing eight different countries (Sweden, Britain, Denmark, France, the Netherlands, Malta, Norway, and Poland; Brady, 2007).

In addition to police-level cooperation, European Interior and Justice Ministers collaborate in the EU's Council of Ministers (JHA Council) to close gaps between member states' criminal laws and legislation to aid cross-border investigation. Using a system of committees and working groups, this multilevel decisionmaking body works to streamline EU rules to facilitate aspects of cross-border justice (e.g., warrants, extradition). Eurojust exists to help implement this coordinated legislation and facilitate multicountry prosecutions. A group of senior prosecutors nominated by member countries, Eurojust has operated since 2003 and has shown rapid caseload growth since its inception (Brady, 2007).

Working in concert with Eurojust is Europol, which is the EU's main tool for combating transnational organized crime. Set up as a hub-and-spoke structure and operational since 1999, Europol gathers, analyzes, and shares intelligence among member states. While it lacks the full operational freedoms of a body like the FBI, it has been granted more operational leeway over the years and can initiate investigation in specific cases and be present during questioning of criminals with advanced permission (Brady, 2007).

The European criminal intelligence model, agreed on by interior ministers in 2005, was initiated as a plan to coordinate investigations against organized crime. Figure 3.2 shows how the model works.

While the systems to enhance intelligence and operational collaboration remain works in progress, at a minimum, the existence of officers from over 25 EU countries working in the same corridor at The Hague is a vital asset to police cooperation.

As in other areas of policing, and life, the informal, personal ties matter more than grander institutional architectures. Those ties will drive policing's future. Police officers will more frequently work across jurisdictions, and the scope of operations granted by one jurisdiction to officers from another will widen. Grand changes in jurisdiction are unlikely, but more-formal institutions will necessarily become more important, despite the difficulties posed by the political nature of those institutions. In some areas, nowhere more than the U.S.-Mexico border, the changes required will amount to redrawing jurisdictions, virtually if not physically. Technology will enable that redrawing. And the evolving criminal threat will require it.

Figure 3.2
European Criminal Intelligence Model

Member-state police forces share intelligence with Europol

Europol draws up assessment of overall organized crime threat

From assessment, Council of Ministers agrees to list of law enforcement priorities

EU police chiefs mount joint operations and feed back lessons learned to Europol

RAND *MG1102-3.2*

CHAPTER FOUR

The Technology Revolution Enables Change

In 1847, Samuel Colt introduced his invention, the revolver pistol, to Captain Samuel Walker of the Texas Rangers, who ordered 1,000 of them for use in the Mexican-American War. Not long after, Colt's pistol replaced the dagger-knife as the country's most popular murder weapon. The pistols also became a standard-issue weapon to police officers in departments nationwide. For a later generation of police officers, the big innovation was the automobile, which vastly extended their range and reach.

This chapter is about technology's potential as an enabler, as well as its potential to stymie departments that are averse to its thoughtful utilization, mostly because they will be left behind in a never-ending game of catch-up. It cannot be stressed enough, however, that technology is an enabler, not a panacea. How it is employed is critical, and those deployments of technology will continue to raise questions of how to balance effectiveness with privacy. At its core, technology has the potential to change (1) data and intelligence gathering, (2) problem-solving processes, (3) partnership structures, and (4) departmental organization. Those technological dimensions will be treated in turn. But first the chapter turns to the challenge of adopting new technology, which is more a matter of concepts of operations than technology per se, and to a look backward at technology's role in making policing what it is today.

The Challenge of Technology

Police departments around the world have been changed by technological advancement ever since the advent of modern policing units. Homicide and sex crime detectives have come to rely on blood, tissue, and hair samples. More recently, they rely on gene typing to determine whether a suspect is the offender in rape cases. Radar has become the major means of patrol enforcement of traffic violations. Patrol officers are linked to mainframe computers permitting online checks for outstanding warrants, stolen vehicles, and the status of motor vehicle registrations and licenses (Reiss, 1992, pp. 83–84).

Until recently, the vast majority of technology adopted by police departments was not invented for police or with the specific aim of improving policing. Rather, the inventors sought to make everyday life easier and richer through innovations ranging from the revolver to the telephone, the automobile to the computer. Yet, it is these developments that have had the most-dramatic impacts on policing organizational structures and operations. If technological advances are rarely made with policing in mind, still, a large number of them have the potential to alter the ways police departments operate. While undisputedly important, technology developed specifically for policing purposes—fingerprinting, the side-arm baton, 9-1-1 systems, riot gear—has also made policing easier but has not changed the fundamental ideas behind policing.

Many of the technologies of the future are already with us or soon will be. If the technological possibilities are legion, so, too, are the anecdotes of how difficult it is to bring those technologies to bear. Partly, policing's emphasis on people, not technology, has left departments with little real capacity to evaluate, or even to understand, what is available. As one senior FBI officer put it, "The Bureau took the dirt road exit from the information superhighway some years ago" (Treverton interview, 2002). Or, as another put it, "The FBI is where the [IBM] 360s go to die" (Treverton interview, 2002). To be fair, the Bureau has since made great efforts to catch up—efforts that, however, display all too vividly the challenge of trying to catch up in big leaps while still remaining short on internal capacity for managing the technological changes.

FBI director Robert Mueller, on the job one week when September 11 occurred, had inherited, along with the terrorism crisis, an FBI whose IT was in a woeful state. Mueller also inherited a major initiative to improve that IT, especially the Automated Case Support (ACS) system, the workhorse database that agents used to store and manage their case files. Yet the designated successor, Virtual Case File (VCF), was still designed for the old FBI, not the new, post–September 11 one. As the National Academy of Sciences panel later put it, "VCF was designed to support the FBI's investigative function. The recently added intelligence mission has significantly different IT requirements and the VCF should not be used as the platform to build those capabilities. An entirely new architecture is needed for this counterterrorism mission" (McGroddy and Lin, 2004).

The FBI was trapped in several kinds of catch-22s. Because it was so far behind in the IT it then needed, the Bureau was tempted to try big—and risky—steps forward. As Darwin John, who was the FBI chief information officer in 2002 and 2003, put it, "In IT, the Bureau was trying to catch up, keep up and position itself for the future all at the same time" (Treverton interview, 2007). The system was all the more complex because it had to handle information at three distinct levels of classification simultaneously—unclassified but sensitive, Top Secret, and SCI. Yet, precisely because the FBI was so far behind in IT, it had to depend heavily on contractors and, moreover, lacked the internal capacity to clearly articulate what it needed and then to manage or evaluate what it got. VCF requirements continually changed over the course of the project, and without a stable, crisp set of technology requirements, the FBI could not require bidders to cost their proposals in ways that could be monitored for compliance. A little more than three years and $100 million later, Mueller cancelled the project (Mueller, 2005).

In other cases, what seems very attractive in principle still runs against the grain of policing practices. In another FBI example from several years ago, a technologically savvy young agent from New York offered headquarters off-the-shelf software for personal digital assistants (PDAs) that would produce near-instant network analysis. Given a name, it would produce everyone that person had been married to, addresses, all the information in publicly available databases—and do so for every agent at a cost in the low tens of millions of dollars. It seemed ideal for an organization that would like its agents out in the field, not sitting at their computers in field offices. And new forms of network analysis are becoming more common. Then, however, it ran afoul of some combination of security concerns and the simple reaction "We don't do things that way."

The challenge of technology, thus, is less technology per se than concepts of operations. The agenda is dramatic. Today, technology companies are strongest at providing technologies. They work with departments to make use of the technology, but primarily from the perspective of what the technologies can do, not what policing requires. Will some private sector organizations become tempted and competent enough to take the next step? Is it imaginable that policing's expanded back office operations might be done by private companies, ones open to and searching for new technologies? Could the oversight and command issues be managed?

Technology and Changes in Policing

Not surprisingly, technology has always been a major driver of policing and police organization. At the turn of the 20th century, policing was organized by walking beats organized into precincts under a local commander (Reiss, 1992, pp. 58–59). By century's end, though, the foot patrol was all but a thing of the past, and most police departments operated from a single headquarters command or, in larger cities, from substation or area commands. What first intervened was the automobile. Motorized patrol supplanted foot patrol. Interestingly, the effect has been more dramatic in the United States. Major cities in Europe but also some in Asia, such as Tokyo, still rely on foot patrol. In the United States, foot patrol is limited, for the most part, to particular business, transportation, or public housing areas.

A second driver of change was communications technology, what we would now call IT. In 1900, the ability to command officers from a central point was very limited, limited literally to the use of a flashing light on a call box, to which the officer could respond only if he could see it. Chicago, for example, installed the Gamewell Police Telephone and Signal Company's Police Signal System in October 1890. In 1893, the department reported that it had 715 call boxes. In 1892, it reportedly handled 4,689,860 duty calls, 61,479 wagon calls, and 2,639 ambulance calls (Hale and Sellers, 1893, p. 222).

So, too, technology afforded supervisory officers only relatively limited means of staying in contact with those in the field they commanded. Corporals or sergeants could move around on foot, bicycle, or horse or in horse-drawn wagon. The advent of radio changed all that, letting supervisors command officers in the field. Later, two-way radios and then handheld ones not only made for easier communication with central headquarters but also with colleagues in the field.

Advancing technology continues to shape the face of policing. Miniaturized recording systems let undercover officers be wired both to record their take and to seek emergency assistance if need be. Computer terminals in their cars, followed by handheld devices, gave officers on patrol access to information systems, enabling them to check quickly for stolen vehicles or outstanding warrants. More and more, officers—like the customer service representative in the vignette with which this book began—will be able to file their reports from their cars or from their handheld devices. They will have the capability to do much of their investigating on the move, all the more so as computer matching of fingerprints and gene types improves. Patrol officers are linked to mainframe computers permitting online checks for outstanding warrants, stolen vehicles, and the status of motor vehicle registrations and licenses (Reiss, 1992). They are trained in identifying intoxicated drivers and in the use of Breathalyzers. In some cities all patrol cars are equipped with fingerprint kits, and police are taught how to use the Automated Finger Print Identification System, a computerized system for matching fingerprint specimens. We will go into more detail on that later.

What is true of general officers is even truer of specialists, across the range. Radar has become the major means of patrol enforcement of traffic violations. Technology is all the more important for those closest to formal trials, such as detectives and evidence technicians. Technology has made detectives less like Sherlock Holmes: They are not out there solving crimes through logical deduction. Indeed, they probably never were. A famous RAND study in 1976 showed that only about 7 percent of detectives' time was spent "solving crimes" (Chaiken, Greenwood, and Petersilia, 1976). There is less "whodunit" and more "what is it?," as they produce evidence on those arrested or suspected. For antinarcotics detectives, that means collecting samples of what may be illicit or controlled substances and submitting them for technical validation before any charges can be made. It also means seeking blood and hair samples. Antinarcotics detectives who make buys to secure a search warrant make use of being wired to secure evidence, as well as to protect themselves. Homicide and sex crime detectives rely on blood, tissue, and hair samples—as well as gene typing—to determine whether a suspect is the offender in rape cases.

The use of technology in the control of crime is by no means limited to detectives. Police evidence technicians now work more closely with fire department specialists in arson investigations. Nor is the use of advancing technology limited to physical technology, for there are parallel developments in adapting advancing social technologies. Perhaps the two that have gained widest adoption in police departments are those of hostage negotiation and special weapons and tactics (SWAT) units. Police share with emergency medical services units the development and use of social and psychological technologies for dealing with suicide attempts.

Technologies on the Horizon

In looking at the horizon, let us consider another vignette. In this case, a police officer arrives at the scene of a domestic violence incident. This time, the officer's en route briefing gives her details on any previous domestic violence at the address, profiles of the couple, whether any weapons have been used, whether weapons are registered at the address, and so on. When she arrives, the wife has been struck several times by her husband, possibly by a blunt object—the officer cannot tell. She and her partners secure the scene and begin their investigation. While her partner interviews the husband, she turns to the wife and asks her to relay what happened. The wife says something in a language the officer cannot understand. The officer pulls up a language detection program on her iPhone and has the wife repeat what she said. The software recognizes the language as Indonesian and begins to translate the wife's words into English automatically. The officer uses her two-way translator to interview the wife about the events, the transcript of which is recorded in real time. The officer takes high-resolution photos of the wife's injuries with her phone.

Meanwhile, her partner gets biometric data from the husband—pictures of his eyes for iris configuration analysis, as well as his whole face for creating a template for facial recognition analysis. The biometric data is sent remotely to the police department's secure computing cloud. While the partner interviews the husband, using the same two-way translator, the geometric configuration of the man's face and irises is calculated, and the results are run through the department's participating databases to see if the husband is involved in other illicit activities.

The statements of both parties are sent remotely to the department's case management system, along with accompanying pictures and the results of the background checks on each of them. The husband will be taken to the station, where he will be held pending assault charges, as well as questioned about an Asian criminal cell with which he has strong ties—a fact turned up by the record search.

This scenario is not one of fantasy. New York and Los Angeles now have "real-time crime centers," which can give a cop who is rolling information about the address, recent calls for service, and recent police activity. While two-way translators are not currently powerful enough to provide real-time translation, they are rapidly approaching this level. Megapixels and cloud computing are becoming increasingly cheap, allowing for the near-instant transfer of precise, unadulterated information from scene to station. Technology has the power to increase the efficiency of police officers, as depicted above, but it also has the power to transform structures of operation, a power that is increasingly being seen as technology in the 21st century continues to radically alter the way police departments collect and process data, solve problems, form partnerships, and, ultimately, structure themselves.

Data Collection and Processing

Walk into one Chicago hotel and your face is instantly captured on camera, but not just any regular camera. The camera uses technology that enables it to make a fully searchable virtual template of your facial features—distance between the eyes, skin pigmentation, hair length and color, orientation of the facial features, and so on. The technology company, 3VR, hopes to become the "Google of surveillance video," letting you simply enter search parameters and watch the results come back. The system is not quite that good, yet. Looking for a person will still generate false-positive results that have to be sifted through, but the technology is here, and advancing. Already, automated license plate readers can constantly scan cars and match them against warrants and stolen vehicles. Faces are bound to come next.

This kind of technology, unprecedented and unimaginable just a few years ago, can have a dramatic impact on the workload of police departments in identifying suspects via video surveillance footage. The searchable data stored by programs like 3VR's could save hundreds of man-hours, freeing up human resources for tasks that computers cannot do. As an example of the potential time savings, a 3VR representative claims that, instead of 1,000 British agents taking six weeks to review surveillance footage leading to the arrest of the 2005 London subway bombers, this technology could have reduced the workload to a dozen agents over the course of a weekend (Vlahos, 2008).

Though "smart cameras" are a dramatic use of technology to increase data collection, other new possibilities for data collection and information processing abound. Global Positioning System (GPS) transmitters have now become inexpensive enough that one department plans to install them on almost everything it can. In one Los Angeles case, a stolen laptop computer was equipped with a GPS transmitter, so police were able to seal off the area to track it down (Gregory Ridgeway interview with Los Angeles Police Department, 2011). Smartphones have GPS transmitters, and even standard cell phones can be tracked via the cell towers through which they are communicating at any given time. In one arson case, police were able to work with the cell phone provider to list all cell phones in the area.

Unmanned aerial vehicles (UAVs) are being introduced to enhance border patrol areas and maintain surveillance of politically and economically strategic areas, such as oil pipelines and national monuments. The military has historically been a testing ground for now-common police technologies, and initiatives by the U.S. military in Iraq and Afghanistan demonstrate the possibilities of UAVs in surveillance and monitoring. New analysts at the National Geospatial-Intelligence Agency (NGA), America's imagery agency, understand that their business has been revolutionized. As one put it, "We used to be looking for things and know what we were looking for. Now we don't know what we're looking for, and we're looking not for things but for activities or transactions" (Treverton interview, 2008).

Their approach is immediately suggestive for policing—if chilling in its possible intrusions into privacy. They seek to geolocate everything that the United States knows about a particular location, from both secret and public sources (Ainsworth, 2008). For example, suppose a UAV with a video camera shows a white truck pulling up in front of a house in Afghanistan. The analysts then would quickly search the database to determine if that arrival might be an activity of interest. If it is, then the activity is the critical bit of information, and all the video footage need not be retained. While the above example may seem advanced—and costly—for mid- and small-sized police departments, consider that the first commercially available microwave sold for between $2,000 and $3,000, but, within about two decades, the cost was reduced by more than a factor of ten. In an era of disposable cameras, the price will approach zero, and cameras can be ubiquitous. In any case, unpiloted drones with cameras will be a less expensive alternative to manned helicopters hovering above crime scenes.

Biometric data for identification is expanding in society and may one day become the norm, making the collection of alternative forms of biometric data important for police organizations. Biometric data can be collected in easier, more cost-effective ways than those currently employed to identify people. Miniature biometric data-collection apparatuses are becoming increasingly cost efficient (Hambling, 2010). "A private vendor, Nanogen, Inc., sells a device the size of a credit card that takes crime scene samples and matches the DNA through a small computer located within a patrol car, supposedly in only a matter of minutes, at a cost of $20 per test compared with current reported costs that range from $600 to $1,600 per test" (Nunn, 2001, p. 12).

Blood samples, iris scans, and DNA typing may come to replace fingerprinting as cheaper, more precise ways of identifying criminals. As well, they may be able to serve as unique identifiers across databases, yielding more accurate cross-database search results. Depending on the level of penetration of biometric data, police may be able to enhance public-private cooperative partnerships as well. It is not impossible to imagine a scenario in which credit card companies turn to a form of biometric identification to fight identity fraud, which police could use to track the spending patterns and locations of suspects more precisely.

Problem-Solving

The massive increase in data collection and storage capability has resulted in an enormous increase in the amount of available information to which police organizations have access when trying to combat crime. Yet, without appropriate tools for organizing, managing, and sifting through these massive amounts of data, the data may drown police, not help them. All that data may do nothing more than require multiple times more man-hours for personnel to cull through the haystacks of data, looking for the needle. More data could simply mean more work, not smarter or more effective policing. Fortunately, improvements in smart-searching and data-sifting technologies are emerging that can help police make sense of their mountains of information in a number of useful ways.

Smart Searches and Pattern-Finding. Police have long known that a relatively small number of people account for a disproportionate amount of crime. As a natural result, increased data collection and analysis seems a natural progression toward greater focus on patterns, behavior, hot spots, and, eventually, on predicting future problems.

The beginnings of data-driven policing can be traced back to the 1990s and New York's CompStat, which sought to provide accurate, detailed, and timely data to assist in police work.

Databases plus models can not only help forecast crimes, which will be discussed in more detail, but models can also be programmed to use crime information to help police pinpoint the location of suspects. Software technology is being developed that can process the seemingly separate pieces of information relating to a crime and connect them in ways that can lead police to the criminal more quickly. For instance, Orange County, California, authorities located a home burglar through the use of geographic profiling software, which uses information about the crimes themselves to suggest potential places where the culprit might live. The software uses crime data, such as locations, suspect information, case details, and investigator details, and then presents those data in two- or three-dimensional surface maps showing the most probable locations of an offender's residence. Using this software, police were able to pinpoint several probable locations of the burglar's residence, and a suspicious person emerged from the shortened list of residences (S. Smith, 2005).

By the same token, the ability of predictive analytics to recognize behavioral patterns is growing rapidly. For instance, these methods can be directed to learn patterns in crime data and search for patterns of similar behavior. These systems are integrated with video surveillance to isolate abnormal behavior in a spatial area (Nunn, 2001, p. 16). The Chicago Police Department attracted a web 2.0 expert to create its Predictive Analytics Group. The group looks for patterns of all sorts. It turns out, for instance, that crime is associated not so much with hot weather as it is with sharply warming weather. So, if next week will bring a 20-degree temperature increase, crime will spike, whether the increase takes the temperature to 90 or only 45 degrees (Gregory Ridgeway interview with Chicago Police Department, 2010).

Not only can cameras hooked up to powerful software detect facial and other identifying features, they can be programmed to "learn" normal human behavior in order to detect unusual or suspicious behavior, such as people standing too close to one another or two people standing at an ATM at the same time, which could indicate that a robbery is taking place. Cameras can be programmed to constantly and quietly monitor activity and then to alert authorities when there is something suspicious that needs to be addressed. In principle, this ability could drastically reduce the man-hours required to monitor risky spaces, freeing up law enforcement and security personnel for other uses—such as community programs, for example.

With the expansion of stored personal data, not just on suspects but on everyone, smart searching is more and more necessary to protect civil liberties and privacy. To cite just one example, Palantir, a company built by former PayPal creators, offers the ability to search large amounts of data while meeting the privacy and civil liberties standards of federal law, as well as those set out in the Markle Foundation Task Force on National Security ("Privacy and Civil Liberties Are in Palantir's DNA," 2009; Markle Task Force on National Security in the Information Age, 2003). It does so by tracking data at a high level of granularity, employing careful core auditing capabilities, and employing a dynamic access framework, which would let leaders in a crisis temporarily expand sharing rules without losing the full scope of protections and audits. It is already in use by some federal agencies and police departments, including LAPD, LASD, and NYPD.

Predictive Policing. Sophisticated predictive models are being developed, often in conjunction with academic and private researchers, that use historical information to forecast where crimes are likely to take place in the future, which can allow police departments to focus their resources in areas most likely to be affected by crime. One of the primary aims is to develop "leading indicator" models, models that can take note of such factors as calls for service, weather, recent disturbances, and school schedules and then anticipate assaults, shootings, retaliations, or the emergence of new drug markets. Early experiences with Memphis's partnership with IBM's Blue CRUSH and Chicago's in-house development of tools indicate that prediction is, while not perfect, better than current practice. The main challenge for predictive policing going forward is whether suitable prevention strategies can be responsive to those predictions.

Data Visualization. While reading a table that displays precincts and the levels of various types of crime within each precinct is useful for determining where crime is occurring with a city, viewing a map of the area with different shading to reflect different levels of crime requires less time to process. Even better still would be a map that could pinpoint crime concentrations down to the block. Scientists long have known that the presentation of information affects one's ability to process and digest the material being presented—a picture is, literally, worth a thousand words. As visually oriented animals, humans, on average, tend to process visual images much more effectively than other forms of information.

This understanding has fueled an explosion of development in the area of data visualization and presentation. Consider the map example above. A software program marries crime report information with GPS data and then, rather than listing a column of numbers, displays this information on a map using data visualization software that shows the information that is important for police managers—car theft is up in area A, and domestic violence is up in area B and down in area C. By way of this technology, police managers can customize a "dashboard" of useful indicators and visualizations that, at a glance, can update them about the status of a topic of interest—all customizable depending on the needs and goals of the manager.

Partnerships

IT, secure protocols and advancements in encryption technology, and applications that enable faster and more open communication between partners have expanded the potential of police departments to engage in collaborative and information-sharing partnerships with external groups—just the sort of proactive collaboration that occurs all too rarely in policing today.

Police-Private Partnerships. The potential for police partnerships with private parties is increased exponentially by the improved data collection ability of private organizations. Police now have unprecedented opportunities for partnering with private security firms; retail and consumer service providers; and other public organizations, such as highway, public safety, emergency management, and fire services, in ways that can improve readiness and responsiveness in both daily operations and emergencies. They might think of some private entities as private analytics partners.

The quasi-alliance that developed in 2010 between Google and the U.S. National Security Agency (NSA), the country's premier eavesdropper and code breaker, is suggestive of the possibilities and also the cautions. Interestingly, in this case it seems to have been Google that turned to the government for help, not the other way around, after Google detected Chinese attacks on its networks (Raphael, 2010; Drummond, 2010). The immediate concerns in this case were whether, in the process of Google getting, in effect, technical assistance from NSA in order to better defend its networks, the government would get access to data from Google users. These concerns were sharpened by the dispute over the Bush administration's authorization, in the wake of the September 11 attacks, of a second track of NSA eavesdropping, called by the administration the terrorist surveillance program (TSP), a track not authorized by the Foreign Intelligence Surveillance Court (FISC) or, indeed, by any other court.

In some cases, private firms are collecting more and better information on the people with whom they interact than do police organizations. Police can leverage this information to aid in criminal investigations, and, increasingly, data collected by private firms can be subpoenaed for trials. Chicago, for instance, boasts a $35 million Citizen and Law Enforcement Analysis and Reporting (CLEAR) system to process all arrests in Cook County for all the departments in real time and grants query access to 450 local, state, and federal law enforcement agencies. The IT unit that handles the system employs 100 staffers and up to 20 contract workers from the system's developer, Oracle. In Edmonton, Alberta, police contracted data analysis technology from Cognos, a business intelligence vendor that is now a part of IBM (Soat, 2009).

To address its shortcomings in video recording surveillance, the Dallas Police Department Narcotics Unit turned to the private sector. A detective from its Technical Operations Unit worked with a local company to devise a new and improved video system. The new video camera was able to send a signal over a secure wireless network, a much-needed improvement from the original microwave technology.

Increasing the optical zoom allowed for greater intelligence both for surveillance purposes and for pre-operations planning. The Dallas Police Department Narcotics Unit is the first law enforcement agency in the country to deploy the camera (T. Anderson, 2010).

As data analysis capability grows in terms of file size and server space, mobility of information means greater use of PDAs, Black-Berries, and cell phones by police officers. Nixle, a community information service, was tested by the Pittsburgh Police Department to facilitate cell-phone communication among its forces during crowd control operations at the time of the September 2009 G20 Summit (Soat, 2009, p. 38)

AT&T partnered with the FBI to allow it access to AT&T's call records after the September 11 attacks. Online retailers keep track of customer purchases, which could be helpful in identifying possible suspicious persons. Police can use these data to gather intelligence and evidence on suspects or to find patterns that appear suspicious. Some firms are creating consumer technology that is uniquely qualified to interface with police. When Mississippi Senator John Burton's Chevy Impala was stolen, he called OnStar. OnStar then called the police. "When officers had the vehicle in sight, they requested that Stolen Vehicle Slowdown be initiated and the vehicle was safely slowed to a stop" (Crofoot, 2010).

Better networking and communication between police departments and other public service agencies can also open pathways for improved performance. Email and niche networking groups among the relevant persons in each organization can allow all organizations to stay alert of events that affect their own operations—road closings, fires, planned drills and exercises, training and community involvement events, and so on. This not only improves the knowledge of police departments but also benefits the public agencies at large.

This chapter has detailed several cases of police departments' use of services and technologies developed by private sector firms to improve their operations. The examples chronicled in this chapter are only a small sampling of the ways in which private organizations are coming to bear on policing. Private firms are now reaching out to police organizations to collaborate on topics of importance to them. Several technology firms and financial companies have regular meetings with police officials in the areas in which they operate in order to keep police abreast of new and emerging trends—for example, in identity fraud. There is some concern that these partnerships, in effect, mean that collaborating companies may get preferential treatment when it comes to investigating crimes. This assertion has not been proven, but it is a cause for concern, and steps should always be taken to ensure the integrity of police departments working with private firms.

Indeed, as policing becomes more data oriented, there is expanding potential—and peril—of contracting out software and data management to private firms, freeing police departments from building their own data and systems infrastructure. Yet, this does not mean that data management operations can be contracted out freely. The use and exchange of possible sensitive personal data on suspects, criminals, and civilians requires a strong commitment to data safety. The increasing interconnectedness of departments brings many benefits but also creates more vulnerability for data to become insecure. It also obscures lines of responsibility for data and information. Data management plans will need to be constructed and implemented to ensure that the information that is being transferred across partnership networks is not compromised.

Police-Community Partnerships. The Boston Police Department has a weblog and a Twitter feed to alert Bostonians to activities of interest and keep them informed of goings-on in the city. Many other departments have also set up community bulletins and Twitter feeds of their own in order to enhance relationships with the community at large. Departments are also utilizing online applications to improve citizens' access to police services, such as filing reports or complaints.

Improvements in technology do not improve only policing. As stressed in this book, the great majority of technology that is revolutionizing policing is also revolutionizing daily life for ordinary Americans. As a result, those citizens themselves have access to technology that can empower them to take a more active role in fighting crime. Citizens can be increasingly proactive in fighting crime by using technology. Most laptops are now sold with a built-in webcam, and users can access their laptops remotely. One woman in Britain whose laptop was stolen turned the webcam on remotely to snap a photo of the thief and then handed the picture over to the police, who successfully tracked down the perpetrator (Leyden, 2008). Police may be able to leverage citizens' access to personal technology by promoting workshops and community programs to inform people of ways that they can help protect themselves or better help the police when a crime does occur—such as spreading knowledge about how to set up a computer for remote access.

With increased community involvement will come increased volume of communication and interaction between police personnel and citizens. This means that the majority of police personnel—not just officers working the street beats—will need training in customer service and client interaction in order to effectively engage the community. It also means that a larger number of personnel within the department may be needed to handle the larger amount of calls, tweets, or online reports and to strategically interface with groups within the community.

Organizational Structure

Functions and Manpower Demands. The changing functions and nature of police work brought on by the adoption and judicious use of technology capabilities mean that manpower demands will also evolve. Future police departments may look less like current ones than the current police chiefs imagine. Police departments that utilize social media and networking tools to interface with the community may require a marketing or social media analyst working in external affairs. An increase in community programs geared toward educating citizens in how to use their personal technology to fight crimes may require a full-time program coordinator and liaison to manage and integrate such programs. Personnel may be needed to manage and sift through an increased number of communications from the community as communication becomes more streamlined and less costly. Along with increased community communication comes the need for police personnel to be more like community service representatives in order to effectively bridge the divide between the department and community.

Internal and External Communication and Collaboration. Technology changes internal communications and organization structures just as much as it has the power to change external communication and operations. The technological ability to secure data transfers, as well as instant message applications, increased bandwidth, niche networking groups, and their kin, all increase the likelihood that partnerships between law enforcement and other public safety agencies can become more integrated and cohesive. This increased level of cooperation has the potential to take place both vertically across levels of hierarchy and horizontally across jurisdictions. According to one assessment, the gaps across jurisdictions, like those detailed in Los Angeles, now can be overcome: "Connecting the department with every other law enforcement agency operating in or around the jurisdiction should be the goal" (Simeone, 2006). The TEW group, described in Chapter Three, is a good example of the type of effective security management that comes out of smart collaboration between law enforcement agencies.

Integrating Technology into Police Departments

In policing, as in other realms of human endeavor, technology for technology's sake is ill advised. Rather, departments will need to consider the suite of technology tools that will best complement their workforce capabilities to meet strategic future needs or goals. Technology is not a single big thing—notice how much trouble the FBI got into when it was driven to try to catch up in IT through one giant leap. Rather, technology is a collection of tools and applications that departments can adopt strategically to achieve their near- and longer-term aims. Nor do different police departments have to adopt the same technological solutions, although in some cases it may be useful to do so for the sake of uniformity or interoperability across departments. The newest and fanciest technologies are not necessarily the most useful or cost-effective for police departments.

If the technological possibilities are legion, so, too, are the anecdotes of how difficult it is to bring those technologies to bear. Partly, policing's emphasis on people, not technology, has left departments with little real capacity to evaluate, or even to understand, what is available. Recall the FBI officer's comment about the Bureau taking the "dirt road exit from the information superhighway some years ago" (Treverton interview, 2002). That action derived, at least in part, from the FBI's emphasis on people, on agents. In other cases, the challenge to be overcome is some combination of security procedures and a "that isn't how we do it" attitude. Recall, on that score, the technologically savvy FBI agent's off-the-shelf software for PDAs that would produce near-instant network analysis, which was not implemented.

With the rapid pace of technological development, it is all too common that "many police agencies now feel they are 'out-tech'd,' not 'outgunned'" (Nunn, 2001, p. 12). Think of the Zetas, who both outgun and out-tech law enforcement. Moreover, there seems to be a general sense of unease when it comes to incorporating new technologies into police departments, one aspect of which is resistance to the idea that technology replaces people. It can do that; yet, without well-trained, smart, concerned police personnel, technology is hardly better. Thoughtful, well-integrated technological solutions should enhance skills, not replace them.

The challenge of technology, thus, is less technology than concepts of operations. The agenda has high stakes. Today, technology companies are strongest at providing technologies, which raises the very real question of outsourcing technology provision and administration to private firms. Will some private sector organizations become intrigued and develop their capabilities to take the next step? Is it imaginable that policing's expanded back office operations might be done by private companies, ones open to and searching for new technologies? Could the oversight and command issues be managed?

In this vein, it is important to remember that technology companies develop technology primarily from the perspective of what the technologies can do, not what policing requires. With that understanding, police agencies will need to have clearly developed ideas of what they need technologies to do that will best complement the skills of their workforce in order to avoid adopting suboptimal technologies. This is all wrapped up in the need for agencies to have vision about future needs. "That wait and respond method of policing is now a thing of the past" (Friedman, 2010). A common theme of this book is the need for agencies to create environments that, culturally and structurally, encourage forward-thinking, proactive responses to shifting trends, rather than waiting for a problem to arise before responding.

The message of this chapter's discussion of technology is that the advances that change the ways in which police departments gather, process, share, and protect data and information are going to have increasingly profound impacts on police organizations. Organizations will become more networked and systems-oriented in a shift toward data-driven policing. As such, data that can be reasonably handled outside of the organization will likely see a move toward outsourcing or backroom operations, as police organizations try to maximize information processing and utilize their human resources efficiently.

To repeat: None of this is to imply that computers, machines, or even outsourced data scientists will replace officers on the force. While the role of technology will grow, the true value of technology is as a complement to human capacity for police work and problem-solving—not a substitute. Police organizations will need to determine their optimal portfolio of technology that works best with the human resources they have available. And, remember, not all technology is useful or appropriate for department functions. Managers will have to exercise prudence and strategic foresight in their technology investment decisions and determine how a technology will improve department operations. What are the trade-offs or risks? What are the alternatives that will also help the department achieve its strategic vision?

CHAPTER FIVE

The Threat Will Continue to Morph

If our world and its technology will not stand still, neither will those of the bad guys. The rapid pace of technological advancement, coupled with more than a century of intense globalization, has led to a highly interconnected world, characterized by the unprecedented movement of goods, services, people, finances, and ideas both across and within borders. These changes have helped to fundamentally alter the nature of the threat to society from crime.

Technological advances; the increasing movement of goods, services, and information; and changing social, economic, and demographic conditions have altered the nature of the crimes, the criminals, and the environment in which criminals and security officers interact. Criminals are committing crimes, such as identity theft, from home that previously required teams of people and intense coordination. Technology-enabled crime has arrived and will continue to develop. And the next step, "virtual" crimes, is not far off; already there are harbingers of that new arena of crime. At the same time, "old" crimes are evolving as to be almost completely distinct from the crimes from which they emerged. In addition, the environment in which criminals operate will morph as technology, law, and law enforcement change. Clearly, none of these dimensions operates independently of the other; they are all interconnected in complex ways.

Criminals take advantage of the opportunities that this new environment affords to commit crimes and, in doing so, shape the environment themselves. Thus, police confront the challenges of a dynamic cycle in which changes in the environment enable new forms of crimes, and, as the criminals adapt, that, too, changes the environment. This chapter discusses ways in which each of these dimensions may change in the future, in order to stress the ever-evolving nature of the crime threat, as well as the importance of law enforcement to understand and anticipate such changes.

Taking Advantage of Seams

Technology enables criminals to take more advantage of the seams in jurisdiction that were the focus of Chapter Three. Consider Russian criminal immigrants to Israel during the 1990s (P. Williams, 2001). With the fall of communism and the collapse in the Russian economy, criminals from the former Soviet Union flooded into Israel, drawn by the law of return, which enabled them to live easily in Israel, and by Israel's lack of anti–money laundering legislation. The techniques were ingenious. Money from Russia would be used to buy virtually bankrupt businesses, which in turn would suddenly become "profitable," with the profits flowing back to Russia. In other cases, criminals would seek to use the vulnerabilities of multiple jurisdictions against them, creating confusion and making it difficult for any given nation's enforcement agencies to target them. The criminals would, for instance, launder money through a series of firms and banks across many jurisdictions, making it arduous and costly for law enforcement to follow the money trail (P. Williams, 2001, p. 71).

Other criminal networks combined Sicilians with Colombians, Colombians with Russians, Turks with Italians, or even more than two groups, such as Calabrians, Turks, and Pakistanis and Colombians, Russians, and Ukrainians. The criminal activities included trafficking in drugs and guns and laundering money (P. Williams, 2001, pp. 76–77). For instance,

> Colombian-Sicilian networks brought together Colombian cocaine suppliers with Sicilian groups possessing local knowledge, well-established heroin distribution networks, extensive bribery and corruption networks, and a full-fledged capability for money laundering (P. Williams, 2001, pp. 75–76).

Italian and Russian criminal networks also found ways to cooperate, while Colombian and Russian criminals met in different Caribbean islands to make deals that exchanged guns for drugs. One indicator that these networks actually worked is the evidence of increased seizures of cocaine imported to or transshipped through Russia. There have also been reports of Colombian money laundering being done in Russia and Ukraine, something that would not be possible without some kind of network collaboration (P. Williams, 2001, p. 76).

The breadth of the networks across very long distances is striking:

> Turkish drug traffickers in Italy [were reported to] have links with the Sicilian Mafia, the Sacra Corona Unita, and the Calabrian 'Ndrangheta. In 1993, a narcotics trafficking network in Turin involved Calabrians, Turks, Pakistanis, and members of the Cali drug trafficking organization, forming what was clearly a highly cosmopolitan criminal network. (P. Williams, 2001, p. 77)

As always, the language needs to be treated with care, and the most overheated of assertions with skepticism. The term *network* is often applied loosely, sometimes meaning true strategic relationships but at other times denoting steady supplier or service contract connections. Virtually all of the networks are marriages of convenience, so some of them may be episodic or fleeting. And *network* connotes a degree of enduring common purpose that may be wide of the mark. Criminal organizations may need help from kindred organizations but wish they did not. Even as they cooperate, they may still be competitors over prices and profits, if not turf.

These networks also reach into the legitimate world to hire lawyers and accountants or financial managers and to bribe law enforcement officers and other government officials (P. Williams, 2001, pp. 79–80). Yet, it was ever thus: The same might have been said of the original Mafia in the United States nearly a century ago. What has changed is less the desire to increase power and decrease risk by developing associates in the non-criminal world than the breadth of the relationships, ones facilitated by all the same technologies, particularly in information but also in moving goods, that have made the licit global economy take off.

As for licit commerce, networking has advantages for criminal organizations, and some of them are the same as for legitimate commerce. Networking, for instance, facilitates access to markets in which the profit margins are largest, and it helps criminals operate from and in countries where risks are the lowest (P. Williams, 2001, p. 78). Networking also makes explicit use of the seams provided by jurisdictions. Committing crimes across borders complicates the tasks of law enforcement agencies that are trying to combat them and can give the criminals flexibility in adapting their methods to counter or neutralize law enforcement initiatives.

Nor need criminal networks be very large to accrue these advantages and, with them, large profits. For Phil Williams, criminal networks of varying "composition, density of connections, size, structure, shape, underlying bonding mechanisms, degree of sophistication, and scope of activities" all can make a lot of money (P. Williams, 2001, p. 84). Criminal networks can have familial bonds, such as with the Cuntrera-Caruana clan, a complex network of blood ties and kinship stretching across industries and geography that also constitutes several important places in the supply chain of Colombian cocaine to Italian distributors (P. Williams, 2001, p. 85). Or they may be bonded by ideology, as was the case when Assad Ahmad Barakat established a lucrative counterfeiting enterprise in the Tri-Border Area of South America to fund Hezbollah and al Qaeda activities (Treverton, Matthies, Cunningham, Goulka, Ridgeway, and Wong, 2009).

Organizationally, a few transnational organized crime syndicates have taken the most steps toward establishing a formal hierarchical structure like that of most legitimate business; the two notorious Hong Kong triads Wo Shing Wo and Sun Yee On are notable examples of this structure (Treverton, Matthies, Cunningham, Goulka, Ridgeway, and Wong, 2009, p. 72). Although logic would suggest that international crime networks require more structure and centrality than domestic or personal criminal networks, especially to be "successful," this is not necessarily the case; a group of eight people who were practically strangers, organized by a Colombian drug trafficker, laundered $70 million by sending large deposits through a simple series of overseas account transfers (P. Williams, 2001, p. 84).

The canonical definition of organized crime comes from the FBI:

> Any group having some manner of a formalized structure and whose primary objective is to obtain money through illegal activities. Such groups maintain their position through the use of actual or threatened violence, corrupt public officials, graft, or extortion, and generally have a significant impact on the people in their locales, region, or the country as a whole. (FBI, undated[b])

Yet, this definition "still retains a tinge of the traditional Mafia about it: There is the suggestion of both geography and hierarchy in the groups" (Treverton, Matthies, Cunningham, Goulka, Ridgeway, and Wong, 2009, p. 14). However, the groups need be neither large nor too sophisticated. "Indeed, the power of small groups in the global economy requires stretching the notion of 'organized.' That power derives from the confluence of technology, networks, and alliances" (Treverton, Matthies, Cunningham, Goulka, Ridgeway, and Wong, 2009, p. 14).

As a United Nations report on counterfeiting describes it:

> The traditional Mafia type organization—which is linked to its territory and which exercises pressing control by means of intimidation and extortion tactics—has gradually expanded to include new opportunities deriving from the globalization of markets and the widespread distribution of technologies. (United Nations Interregional Crime and Justice Research Institute, 2007, p. 104)

According to Treverton, Matthies, Cunningham, Goulka, Ridgeway, and Wong (2009, p. 14):

> Trade in narcotics and contraband products required a move away from hierarchy toward alliances with other groups across the globe. Crime became transnational. Moreover, with the coming of the digital age, IT allows operations to shrink what IT specialists call the "minimum sustainable scale of operations." That is true for commerce, especially the huge "virtual" market of the Internet. It is also true for illicit commerce, perhaps especially for

crimes where the barriers to entry are relatively low. Small groups can make major money—and cause major mayhem.

Nor do they have to be large to make use of the seams created by different and geographically denominated jurisdictions.

Technological Advances

All our lauded technological progress—our very civilization—is like the axe in the hand of the pathological criminal—Albert Einstein, 1917 (Dukas and Hoffmann, 1981, p. 88).

Technology-enabled crime (TEC) refers to crimes committed using increasingly sophisticated technology and technological skill. TEC includes cyber crime and cyber terrorism, discussed in the next section; new crimes evolved through technology from old ones; and a realm of virtual crimes, a world into which police are only beginning to venture. Non–cyber crime TEC takes place in the physical world as technology aids or facilitates the crime. This includes crimes using high technology, like the skimming example above in the next section. It also includes using technology, especially the Internet, to link criminals to victims or to facilitate criminals' perpetration of crimes in the real world.

Technology-Enabled Crime and the Internet

Even without the Internet, technology has enabled crime to evolve and will continue to do so. Criminals are often the first adopters of new technologies and use them to their advantage to thwart law enforcement. For example, drug dealers were very quick to adopt pager and cell-phone technology in the early to mid-1990s. The technology was perfect for their purposes. When GPS was still a nascent technology, drug smugglers used tiny GPS-enabled "bugs" to track their shipments via cell phone, as well as to receive alerts if the shipment was diverted in transit or picked up by authorities (Helm, 2001).

Today, commonly available technology is allowing criminals to inject a high level of sophistication into criminal activities. Crimes using technology are becoming more prevalent, and more frightening, as people are less able to take measures themselves to confound criminals. Imagine going to an ATM to withdraw money, as millions of Americans do every day. As you enter the ATM kiosk, another person walks in behind you. As a conscientious user, you keep an eye on her, just in case, and are sure to keep the keypad covered as you punch in your PIN. On leaving, you take your receipt with you, just in case someone decides to go digging in the trash can near the ATM for it. You walk out of the kiosk, knowing that you did the best you could to prevent your account from being compromised.

What you did not know was that the woman you were careful about was not the threat. The real person you needed to be worried about was in a sedan around the corner. He had installed a "skimmer" device and a micro-camera in the ATM yesterday. The skimmer looks so similar to the real faceplate of the ATM that you did not notice it as it read your account number when you inserted your debit card. The camera that was nestled in a box containing pamphlets captured your PIN, even as you covered it from sight of the person behind you. Made from spare cell phone parts, the skimmer and camera transmitted your account number and video of your PIN to the sedan. The criminal will now go back with a replica of your debit card and empty your account.

The Internet does not just give rise to cyber crime. Its ability to facilitate non–high-tech crime is almost as striking. Prostitution is a notorious example. Websites, such as Craigslist, allow users to post classified ads, much like those in a community newspaper, for free. Although Craigslist and other sites explicitly prohibit the use of their sites for such purposes, the "adult" sections of the site are awash with advertisements by prostitutes for sex, usually in coded language. Law enforcement has been able to use Craigslist to increase the number of sting operations it conducts against prostitutes and johns, but it is unable to keep up with the sheer volume of exchanges. Sometimes these encounters can turn from vice crimes into violent ones. Phillip Markoff, the "Craigslist killer," met three women who were offering erotic services on Craigslist in 2009. Markoff robbed all of them and murdered one (Huff, 2009).

As people connect more frequently with strangers, either socially or for economic exchange, the Internet is becoming a way for violent criminals to connect with victims. In early 2010, Jim Sanders listed a diamond ring for sale on a classifieds page. He arranged a meeting with a potential buyer at his house to inspect the ring, but this turned out to be three men and a woman who beat his wife and shot and killed him before absconding with the ring and several other valuables (Karlinsky, Miller, and Ferran, 2010). Katherine Olson was murdered in Minnesota in 2007 when she arrived at what she thought was a babysitting job that she had arranged online (Nauert, 2007).

With the rise of social networking sites, such as Facebook, stalking also has become an issue of major importance. Now stalkers can easily track their victims from afar to an unprecedented degree. This includes violent criminals stalking their future victims. The lack of privacy and the ubiquitousness of personal information on the Internet allows criminals unprecedented access to victims' personal lives, including information on their daily schedules, workplaces, interests, families, and friends.

Moreover, the web can allow almost-complete anonymity. Users are able not only to hide their true identities but can also adopt names and personas that are completely disconnected from their physical identities. This is a particularly troublesome development when a child molester can enter a chat room pretending to be a 13-year-old and proceed to chat up other teenagers for the purpose of engaging in online sex—or meeting them in real life in the future. Moreover, it is more difficult to prosecute people for child exploitation if they can claim that they thought that the person on the other end of the conversation was also an adult who was merely role-playing. The anonymity of the Internet confounds law enforcement's attempts to investigate and prosecute these types of crimes to a degree never experienced before.

The rise of the Internet and the democratization of commerce also mean that there are fewer ways to make sure that pirated or counterfeit goods are not infiltrating the online marketplace. Indeed, they are. Here, *democratization* means the expansion of commercial capabilities to a larger number of people. The barriers to buying and selling have been reduced by the Internet such that literally anyone with an Internet connection can be a seller of goods across the globe. In a personal experience, one of the authors ordered the second season of a popular HBO show from a third-party retailer, hosted by the popular site Amazon.com. Amazon is a well-respected, legitimate online retailer, and the item description gave no indication that the DVDs would be anything other than authentic. Yet, what came in the mail was a clearly pirated version of the DVD in non-English packaging, complete with poor-quality English subtitles.

The Internet has clearly altered the way people interact socially, politically, and economically. It also has widespread ramifications for the way criminals operate. Indeed, above and beyond the examples listed in the previous sections, technology and the Internet have given birth to a whole new breed of crime—cyber crime.

Cyber Crime

Cyber crime is a special genre of TEC. Rather than using technology to facilitate the perpetration of real-world crimes, cyber criminals perpetrate crimes almost entirely using technology and the Internet. The most prevalent cyber crimes are identity theft and the theft of sensitive personal information, fraud, money laundering, and cyber attacks for political or economic gain. Yet, cyber criminals also engage in a number of other criminal activities.

As Internet use becomes ever more widespread, more valuable information and assets are stored electronically, and the benefits to crime using technology are ever-increasing. As of 2009, an estimated 27.3 percent of the world's population (1.9 billion people) had access to a personal computer at home ("World Telecommunication/ICT Indicators Database 2010," 2010). Cyber crime is the fastest-growing component of crime in the world. The likelihood of suffering from a "real" crime in the physical world is now lower than that of being the victim of a virtual crime. "Committing cyber crimes is much more profitable, significantly less risky, and strictly linked to market logic and trends" (Buddenberg, 2010).

Many cyber crimes are crimes that have evolved via technology from "old" crimes—money laundering, identity theft, fraud, and extortion, to name several of those most commonly discussed. Yet, if they are the present-day versions of their predecessors, these cyber crimes have diverged to such an extent from the crimes from which they evolved that they can no longer be arguably related to their parent crimes. For one thing, the scope of these crimes is on a scale incomparable to their predecessors. Small operations or even individuals themselves can illegally acquire large amounts of personal data, money, or other sensitive information for economic gain. Again, it is the IT principle of decreasing minimum scale of sustainable operations on display.

In the largest case of identity theft so far prosecuted, hacker Albert Gonzalez broke into the electronic files of TJX, a large discount retailer, and siphoned off over 90 million credit card numbers from the company over the course of eight months, resulting in $200 million in losses (Zetter, 2010). In the case of identity theft and fraud, crime in the cyber world allows talented individuals to do what previously required major orchestrations by criminals in the physical world.

Extortion and cyberattacks are also a major area of concern. Criminal organizations have turned to cyber extortion as a way to extract protection money from businesses with online presence. Generally, these take the form of a distributed denial of service (DDoS) attack, a tactic in which hackers use thousands of computers connected to the Internet to deluge a company's website with bogus communications, overloading the company's servers and shutting out legitimate users' activities. Hackers threaten companies with DDoS attacks unless they transfer money to the hackers. In an infamous recent case of this kind of extortion, before Super Bowl XXXVIII hackers threatened to shut down several online betting sites before and during the game, potentially costing them tens of millions of dollars in lost betting revenue (O'Connell, 2008). These types of situations, in which hackers exploit system weaknesses in return for protection money, are becoming more and more common. Yet, they are also difficult to combat, as companies are reluctant to share information or divulge that they have been the target of cyber extortion, fearing that they will lose customers as a result.

Cyber crime has evolved drastically in less than ten years. Gone are the days when amateur hackers were more spelunkers than criminals, gaming the system "just to see what happens." Expert hackers are cashing in on their technological skill in an eerie specialization of labor in the market for cyber crime tools. High-level hackers have become suppliers of sensitive information, computer programs and packages, and other tools that end users need to carry out criminal enterprises. This activity has become so advanced that online marketplaces have sprung up where criminals can literally shop for batches of stolen credit card numbers and other identifying information, bank account numbers and passcodes, and skimming devices, as well as botnets (networks of computers that are used for malicious purposes without their owners' knowledge) and trojans for spam attacks. Even more frustrating is the fact that these criminals can adopt innocuous personas in real life; the founder of DarkMarket, the best known of these marketplaces, was a pizza bar worker (Davies, 2010). DarkMarket was busted in 2010.

The tactics of cyber criminals also are evolving. High-level cyber criminals are becoming subject-area experts. They may become highly knowledgeable about the intricacies of a single, large company and devote their time and energy to infiltrating the security of that single firm. With large firms, this payoff can be quite sizable. EBay has struggled for years with a single "specialist" hacker, known only as Vladuz (Bradbury, 2007). Additionally, spam and scam attacks are being directed more intensively than in previous years. Rather than sending scam emails to as many recipients as possible, spammers and would-be scammers are focusing on a select few more intensely, such as the executives of companies, with emails they might actually expect to see in their inboxes (Timson, 2010).

The ultimate frustration with cyber crime was probably put best by U.S. Deputy Secretary of Defense William Lynn: "[A] missile comes with a return address, a computer virus generally does not" (Lynn, 2010). Cyber criminals are often known only by their handles, or aliases, and are skilled at keeping their physical and virtual identities distinct. Law enforcement will likely deal with more of these types of criminals as human capital in technology progresses.

Virtual Crimes and Real Crimes in Virtual Worlds

As people spend more time online, they establish virtual identities that may or may not be similar or related to their physical identities. Indeed, people often take pains to hide their physical identity. An intelligence analyst, for instance, seeking to protect his professional identity, may state that he is a martial arts expert in his virtual persona. An increasing number of social, economic, political, and cultural interactions take place online, creating opportunities for new crimes to be perpetrated against our virtual selves.

One area where new crimes are emerging is in massive multiplayer online games (MMOGs). World of Warcraft (WoW), Runescape, and Second Life are notable MMOGs in English-speaking countries, and QQ is currently the most popular one in China. Users create avatars to represent themselves in order to interact in these virtual worlds. Inside these virtual platforms, users can socialize via real-time voice chat, start a business or work for income, and buy and sell goods and services. Indeed, arguably, anything that can be done in real life can be done in an MMOG, and sometimes even more than in real life, in the sense that the worlds created have many fantasy characteristics, and users can create avatars that are not only a different gender or age but even a different species.

Along with the popularity of these platforms has come the widespread use of virtual currencies created by the game designers for use within the system. Because of the value of the virtual currency to the players, several virtual currencies have exchange rates with real-world currencies. Some currencies are actually sold at a set price by the manufacturer. One QQ coin, produced by Tencent Corporation, retails for one Chinese renminbi, or about $0.13 USD (Wang and Mainwaring, 2008). Others, such as WoW gold, are explicitly stated to be only for use in the game, not as a form of currency for real economic exchanges, yet they are traded on several unregulated third-party websites. As such, the exchange rate is neither constant nor uniform. At one site, 500 WoW gold coins ranged from $11–17 USD (Internet Game Exchange, 2011).

Because of the real-world value of virtual currencies, criminals are taking advantage of new opportunities for money-laundering schemes, using illicit funds to purchase virtual currencies and then exchanging them again for legitimate, real-world currency. Even outside of virtual worlds, other virtual currencies, such as e-gold, are used to launder money and act as currency in a number of the illicit marketplaces mentioned above. E-gold, an anonymous online currency, was the currency of choice for some members of Shadowcrew, a global crime forum. One member reportedly laundered between $40,000 and $100,000 each week for the organization from his California home (Solomon, undated). The unregulated financial sectors appearing in virtual spaces are real concerns for law enforcement investigating the movement of illicit funds.

Not only are real-world crimes taking place in virtual worlds, but, as people's identities become less dependent on their physical existence and become more wrapped up in these virtual worlds, there is the question of whether crimes against people's virtual selves are, in fact, actual crimes. Some analysts looking into the future of crime on the Internet, as well as the role of virtual worlds, have already proposed this as a real and growing problem (Schafer, 2007; Choo, Smith, and McCusker, 2009; Buddenberg, 2010). And, far-fetched as it seems, it already has happened. The widely known first case of "virtual" rape occurred in New York in 1993, and the most widely known case thus far reported to the police was in 2007 by a woman in Belgium (Clark-Flory, 2007). Now, this issue is certainly no priority when there are so many real rapes to prevent and solve, but it shows how quickly the distinction between real and virtual is eroding, and it raises at least the possibility that police may confront people who want retribution for crimes against their virtual selves.

Social, Demographic, and Economic Shifts

Social shifts breed new types of crimes. Examples are the rise in the late 1990s and early 2000s of teenage school shootings and violent road rage incidents. The online presence of young people and democratization of knowledge means that everyone is on the Internet and broadcasting themselves. In perhaps the ultimate paradox of changing social mores, a 15-year-old Ohio girl was arrested in 2008 for sending nude photos of herself to other minors. She faced felony criminal charges for illegally using a minor in nudity-oriented material and for possession of criminal tools. If convicted, the teen could have been forced to register as a sexual offender annually for ten years. In the end, she reached an agreement with prosecutors and did not have to register as a sex offender (Zetter, 2008).

In addition to technology, society and economy are ever in flux, meaning that trends in more traditional types of crime will change, as well as the relative prevalence of these types of crime. Migration and other demographic shifts influence the types of crimes that police departments find themselves responding to as much as technological shifts. Fortunately, these crimes seem more predictable than TEC and cyber crime. Still, law enforcement will need to evaluate the potential of emerging social and economic trends to alter the crime topography, as well as consider ways to preemptively counteract those effects. According to Schafer (2007, p. 31):

> While the overwhelming majority of immigrants will be law abiding, obvious challenges for the police include immigrant criminal gangs, closed and distrustful communities, imported ethnic rivalries and feuds, different types of crime (e.g., human trafficking), and a lack of understanding with regard to host country laws and customs.

Moreover, the increasing international connectedness of criminal organizations allows them opportunities to use alternative languages for communication in order to sidestep U.S. officials. As migration from Mexico continues, particularly as criminal flows continue to filter into the southern United States, law enforcement may need to make aggressive efforts to increase its number of bilingual officers. Forecasted trends in migration from eastern and Northern Africa also highlight a potential need for law enforcement to develop a capacity with these languages.

The number of elderly people in the United States is also a factor to consider. Larger aging populations pose new concerns and challenges for police organizations. As populations age, police departments are likely to receive more calls for help regarding crime that is both real and perceived—for instance, items merely mislaid but perceived as stolen. And those calls will more and more often concern victimizations employing technology with which the elderly victims are unfamiliar, or even types of crime that are new to them. On the plus side, elderly persons are also more likely to be community organizers and involved in their local and community government. As a result, police departments may be able to recruit older people to be partners of the department. Elderly people may be enticed to organize neighborhood watches, run and administer education programs, or engage in community outreach and customer service relations within the community. Police departments will want to think about populations within their own community to whom they can reach out and with whom they can build relationships.

Increasing Movement of Goods, Services, and Information
The massive increase in the volume of transported goods caused by the dismantling of trade barriers and the expansion of global trade has made it easier to hide contraband goods in the miasma of goods that flow through relatively open borders 24 hours a day.

In this environment in which goods, services, and money flow so easily, criminal organizations are becoming increasingly international. Trade routes represent not only an opportunity for consumers to benefit from trade but also an opportunity for criminals to exploit cost-saving strategies and jurisdictional limitations of local law enforcement to thwart detection. Like many legitimate businesses, criminal organizations are also tending to shift their operations overseas or across jurisdictions in order to benefit from division of labor savings and to avoid detection—a major theme of Chapter Three. They also benefit from the increased volume of trade to move illicit goods (and people) across borders unprotected. The limited resources of customs officials and other law enforcement means that not even close to all of the material that is sent through ports and transit routes can be inspected.

As international money flows bulge, "[T]he boundaries between criminal syndicates, terrorist groups, and gangs will continue to disappear. Alliances between seemingly disparate and unrelated organizations should be expected" (Schafer, 2007, p. 32). Criminal organizations act to maximize the bottom line. As trade flows increase and criminal organizations begin to operate more like businesses to maximize profit, they are increasingly outsourcing some of their operations to terrorist organizations, as in the Tri-Border Area of South America. Terrorist organizations, needing money to finance their campaigns, have an opportunity to raise funds by engaging in counterfeiting, drug trafficking, and the movement of goods and people across borders, either for themselves or for criminal organizations. Third-generation gangs engaged in narcotics trafficking, as well, are becoming increasingly violent with other gangs over control of smuggling routes and with law enforcement as they crack down on the drug trade.

The More-Distant Future Will Manifest New Challenges

According to Newton's Third Law of Motion, for every action there is an equal and opposite reaction. For law enforcement, this means that changing legal priorities or law enforcement strategies will spur criminals to exploit relative weaknesses elsewhere as a way to mitigate risk. If law enforcement cracks down on crime in Area A, then crime in Area B becomes relatively more profitable. For example, tighter restrictions on the sales of pseudoephedrine—the drug in decongestants and wakefulness-promoting agents, but also a constituent ingredient in illegal methamphetamines—has largely driven production of methamphetamines from America's rural South and Midwest to Mexico. Consequently, there has been an increase in the flow of methamphetamines across the southern border, as well as increased gang activity by the organizations that traffic and distribute the drugs (National Drug Intelligence Center, 2010). Before that, clamping down on drug smuggling routes through the Caribbean shifted cocaine and other drug traffic to routes through Mexico—the backdrop to the enormous rise in drug-related crime in Mexico.

Technological progress will continue to advance, likely well beyond the realm of what we currently imagine possible. With this progress will come new opportunities for criminals to thwart law enforcement. Criminals are often the first adopters of new technology precisely because it is new and law enforcement will thus be unfamiliar with its potential uses, giving criminals the edge: Witness the FBI's dirt-road exit from the information superhighway. How will the rise of cloud computing change the ways that criminals move money or the ways that political groups establish presences in the virtual realm? Already visible is the impact on searches. If police seize a suspect's computer, can they legally open and search any application? The personal information of interest about the suspect will be somewhere, but it may be in the cloud (or even stored for convenience by the service provider on someone else's computer). Is that information still fair game? How will law enforcement deal with the emerging issues connected with nanotechnology and human privacy as it becomes embedded in more direct-to-consumer technology? How will new technology help law enforcement, as well as help criminals?

Whatever technologies emerge in the future, the "early adopter" phenomenon is a trend among certain criminals, and law enforcement will need to be aware of the possible criminal uses of nascent technologies, as well as develop protocols for dealing with technological evidence. Before standards were developed for handling cell phones by police agencies, officers would sometimes turn them off to save battery life, which could sometimes erase the call log and text message history, resulting in a loss of potential evidence (Helm, 2001). Policing will need to adjust to these issues; as seen in the case of the TEW and the anthrax cases in Chapter Three, thinking about adverse events before they happen can help law enforcement develop a timely and appropriate response to be used when they finally arrive.

As the world evolves, so will crime and the individuals who engage in it. Not least, "physical boundaries will be replaced by electronic and philosophical ones as individuals discover new virtual communities" (Schafer, 2007, p. 33). Law enforcement's task in the future will be to keep abreast of changes and to forecast and prepare for likely changes before they happen. Playing a reactive game will not work in a future where the pace of technological and societal change is always increasing. Playing a proactive role may include the increasing sophistication of predictive crime models and crime mapping or the use of political and economic expertise to forecast demographic trends and anticipate how those trends will affect crime rates. It will probably also include having a more global perspective in its operations, and that will be the case not just for large agencies. Small agencies, too, will need to be aware of events well beyond their jurisdictions to be able to depict and predict patterns that affect their constituents.

In short, law enforcement will need to learn to predict, and possibly preempt, much of criminal activity. If technology will not stand still, neither will the bad guys. In a globalized world, they will have access to virtually every weapon and technology that the good guys know. Technology will not defeat them; that will take dramatically improved concepts of operations. The targets of crime will be where the money is. Yet, three features of tomorrow's threat are clear. First, what specialists say about IT is also true of crime: The minimum sustainable scale of operations is diminishing. The Mafia was a hard target but a large one. Now and into the future, technology empowers small groups to commit major crime. Second, the boundaries between criminal, terrorist, and insurgent organizations are blurring, again frustrating familiar policing categories and practices. Finally, the criminal groups will be loosely networked in new and changing ways. When police practice changes in one part of the globe, criminals in other parts will know as quickly as the police do.

CHAPTER SIX

Concepts of Operations Are Critical

If the technologies are now with us or soon will be, the critical challenges are operational, what are called concepts of operations, or ConOps. Some are trivial but could be important, like the change of titles in the introduction's vignette, from "officer" to "customer service representative." Others are practical, like finding resources to deploy today's technology rather than having to live with the previous generation's. Another set of challenges runs to the culture of police organizations. When asked what their police forces will look like in 20 years, police chiefs almost always say "much like now," though with changes in gender and ethnicity proportions. Yet, surely those future forces will differ in skill set as well. But how different? Might the balance tip sharply from those customer service representatives on the street toward those who build and operate tomorrow's versions of computers in the back office, from officers toward analysts? Might deterring crime rest less on physical presence than on an increased chance of being caught?

Beyond the cultures of police organizations, there is the wider American political culture in which policing is embedded, a point that is a theme of this book. While technology enables, it takes changes in organizational practice and culture to make use of those enablers. And those changes need to be blessed—or at least accepted—by American society. On the one hand, technologies, like those described in Chapter Four, are dramatically reshaping what privacy means, almost without Americans noticing it.

Yet, on the other, there surely will be specific backlashes against the use of certain technologies in certain ways—witness, for instance, the backlashes in some states against fixed cameras catching speeders, or against Facebook when, in late 2009, it moved to make public users' information that previously could be restricted. It remains to be seen whether there will be a more general and sustained backlash against what is, in historical terms, such a dramatic change in privacy. Yet, because policing is sensitive in any case, citizens are likely to be more sensitive about its practices than Facebook's. And even without a sustained backlash, concern over specific technologies used in particular ways is sure to affect not only the pace of change in policing but also the consistency of that change across different jurisdictions.

How Might Operations Change in the Future?

Policing is ever-evolving. Although the pace at which technology, criminal activity, and other threats continues to morph may seem daunting, that means that adaptations in policing practices must be just as fluid. Chapter Two illustrated the adaptability of policing. As challenges have arisen, whether due to internal problems, societal expectations, or new technologies, policing practices have changed as well. For instance, in reaction to the public disillusionment about police corruption of the political era, the reform era witnessed the establishment of objective decision rules and top-down restructuring of the force. When it became clear that the "objective" and hands-off policies of the reform era were ill suited to deal with the political turmoil of the 1960s, policing evolved again.

The community and problem-solving era increased police connections to the local community not only to garner popular support for the police forces writ large but also to build partnerships in preventing and apprehending crime. This era also saw the development of social experiments and academic policing scholarship. Both were aimed at understanding the effectiveness of current policing practices and how to make them even better. With the development of new technologies, communications and otherwise, ILP and practices supported by empirical analysis have replaced some of the previously held beliefs about how to best prevent and apprehend crime. Although laying out a precise blueprint for how ConOps will have to change would be presumptuous at best, and futile at worst, it is possible to identify the issues that will need to be considered.

First, objectives of policing will change as the nature of crime changes. The overall goal of policing, the prevention and apprehension of crime, will, of course, remain the same. However, as theories develop over how to best achieve this outcome, changes in the operational objectives of policing will follow. Take, for instance, the differences in policing that occurred as a result of the transition from the reform era to the community policing era. The objectives of the reform era included impartial policing, standardization of practices, and also the professionalization of the force. After the broken windows theory developed, and OMP surfaced as a result, the objectives of the community policing era shifted. Instead of focusing on crime apprehension, police focused their efforts on creating environments that were less conducive to crime. Involvement with the neighborhood and development of relationships with key players in the community were key objectives of policing during this era. As policing now transitions to the ILP era, operational objectives have shifted once again. Collecting data and using the findings of analysts to improve policing practices have defined the operational objectives of today.

Of course, as said often in this book, there are no sharp delineations of when objectives change or policing practices transition between eras, or even how those practices develop within each period. For instance, although policing is now shifting toward ILP, involvement in the community remains an important focus of policing. Unfortunately, competition for resources—whether money or the time and attention of leaders—makes considering the trade-offs between pursuing differing objectives critical. For instance, community involvement and police presence itself can be made manifest at very different levels of intensity. One precinct may choose to focus 40 percent of its resources on supporting this endeavor, while another may choose to invest almost 100 percent of its forces in developing community relations. Each of these choices requires that the appropriate training programs and supporting infrastructure be established. Each officer that is employed on the beat in a neighborhood is one that cannot be at the office figuring out patterns of criminal behavior.

The trade-offs are even clearer between community-based policing and the transition to ILP. Similar to the policies instituted during the reform era, ILP focuses on uniformity in policing practices. This is in stark contrast to community-based policing, which gives individual policemen and policewomen latitude to make decisions based on their individual knowledge of a particular neighborhood or population. However, it is still unclear what combination of these strategies of policing is the most effective. At what point, for instance, will policing become *too* dependent on analytical techniques? Analytical techniques are important but should only aid in making decisions; they surely cannot replace the human element. Similarly, how much should police stay involved in the neighborhood communities? The community is necessary to preventing crime, not least of which because they supplement limited police resources. However, personal ties risk clouding objective decisionmaking and often prevent the force from understanding the big picture or relationships between individual events.

Policing theory will surely continue to develop. It is still unclear whether deterrence by presence, OMP, or even ILP are the best methods by which to keep society safe. Studies and scholars continue to disagree about whether focusing on preventing crime or apprehending criminals is more effective in reducing crime rates. In addition, policing is only one component of the overall criminal justice system. As the legal system and the level of punishment for different types of crime change, there will likely be shifts in policing. This is true of the new developments in crime as well. For instance, the increasing prevalence of cyber crime demands that operational objectives related to this avenue also develop. New objectives may include increased surveillance online or faster response times to identified threats. Similarly, as crime becomes more globalized, operational objectives focused on communication and information-sharing will need to develop.

Changing Organizations

As policing ConOps change, a restructuring of command structures may also be necessary. Unsurprisingly, for policing as for other areas of governance, there is no obvious "best" organization. We are and always will be in the process of discovering what works better. Policing in the United States has shifted between horizontal and more vertical decisionmaking structures. The political era of early America remains the most decentralized model of policing—because of both the lack of technology available at the time and the political connections that granted police their law-enforcing authority.

At the other end of the spectrum, the organization of the police force during the reform era was extremely centralized. Top-down decisionmaking replaced the latitude previously given to individual police officers. This transformation was also enabled by the widespread use of standardized guidebooks for policing practices and the ability to communicate and coordinate via technological advancements, such as the radio. Although the two more recent eras of policing, community policing and ILP, recognize that both the extreme decentralization and centralization of earlier policing eras are unwise, they still lie on opposite ends of the organizational spectrum.

From a purely organizational perspective, centralized and decentralized structures have both benefits and drawbacks. Horizontal organization of policing allows for quicker response and more tailored approaches to problems that surface. The benefits of this approach inspired the organizational changes during the community policing era. Instead of using a rule book to dictate every aspect of police behavior, each officer was given leeway to make decisions based on his or her own judgment and understanding of the local population's needs and characteristics. Policing of this era recognizes that situational awareness is necessary for effective crime prevention and apprehension. Bearing in mind the diversity of the neighborhoods in large cities such as New York City, Los Angeles, or Chicago drives home the importance of tailor-made approaches. Each neighborhood not only has its own local population dynamics to consider, but often unique criminal characteristics as well. A one-size-fits-all policy is almost guaranteed to fail.

Yet, that does not imply that there is nothing to be said for more centralized decisionmaking models. Vertical organization of power makes it easier to hold police practices to a high standard and enables communication and coordination between different officers. The ILP era reaps the benefits of a more centralized organizational structure. As crime becomes more globalized, crossing city, county, state and country lines, facilitating the sharing of information-sharing across units and precincts is imperative. Without some standardized practices, even in matters as small as the way police record crime-related data, coordination and information-sharing will remain a fairly theoretical proposition. Even more practically, the lack of some standardized practices makes evaluating police activities impossible. In a day and age where data and research drive new policy decisions, understanding what works and what does not is critically important to improving policing practices. In addition, criminologists are recognizing more and more that patterns exist in criminal activity. Being able to make widespread changes to police practices based on newly identified blueprints or modus operandi will continue to improve the effectiveness of police forces.

Decisionmaking structure is not the only organizational consideration for the future of policing. Whether the specialization of police forces, epitomized through the various task forces that exist today, will continue to be necessary in the future remains to be seen. The recognition that generalists and specialists are both needed skill sets on any team is uncontroversial but also not very helpful. What may be the case is that, as police departments find better ways to survey the population and facilitate the flow of information, the balance in the number and the emphasis on specialists may change. One future that can be imagined is one in which most in-house specialists are replaced by databases of criminal, forensic, and other information.

On the other hand, another imaginable future would hold more specialists with deeper understanding of their subject matter, experts who are regularly consulted either to solve criminal cases or to help formulate solutions to recurring problems. In both futures, how policing units across the United States relate to each other in the future will require significant consideration. Especially in the age of ILP, the sharing of information between and across various jurisdictions can aid in the prevention not just of crime but also of terrorism. How the forces can reorganize in the face of turf wars between different offices is a challenge faced by organizations at all levels of public service in the United States.

New Workforce Demands

New developments in policing methods will demand changes in the police workforces. Considerations include not only the necessary changes in personnel requirements but also the training programs and recruiting practices that support them. The workforce demands of the specialized task forces of today demonstrate the variety of considerations for future policymakers in this regard. The point is driven home, interestingly, by the host of crime shows on television. In the various *Law and Order* series, the focus on anthropologists, forensic specialists, or even psychology profilers gives average Americans their pick of criminology entertainment. Each of these approaches requires highly educated professionals to fulfill certain niches in the crime-fighting team.

Although in reality these teams are less autonomous than they appear on TV, often working in conjunction with other specialists and teams on a case, they are still a reality of policing today. One of the most famous of the functional specialties is the terrorism task force of the NYPD. The training and demand for these police officers varies substantially from the police forces in downtown Detroit, for instance. However, despite the prestige of the NYPD terrorism task force, whether or not it makes sense for a similar task force to exist in every city is a consideration to be made. One thing remains clear: As the faces of crime change, so too will the team of police that apprehends them.

As mentioned earlier, the necessity for task forces may decrease as community-based policing shifts toward ILP. This, in and of itself, holds its own workforce considerations. Will specialists be replaced by communications officers? Will these communications officers be supported by a new IT staff that can navigate through the databases and troubleshoot problems associated with new software? In what capacity will analysts be used, and how many will be needed to support each precinct? All of these questions have different answers—all of which could be correct, given the face of crime in the future.

One possibility for the future workforce is the model of the federal world of intelligence. Both the Central Intelligence Agency (CIA) and the FBI, for instance, are home to both agents that collect data and conduct operations and to analysts that process the data and support the activities of the agents. Another innovation, one in open source intelligence production, is especially suggestive for policing, though it is not so easy to see how it could be scaled up in size. Open Source Works, a CIA organization, consists of about 100 analysts, none of whom has a security clearance and half of whom work in the language they spoke while growing up. It also locates its technical people right in the middle of the analysts, so that technical problems can be solved on the fly. ILP seems to be progressing toward these intelligence models. If so, however, the recruiting, training, and retention of these forces will look very different from the practices of today.

As police departments collect more personal and potentially sensitive data, they will need to protect the integrity and security of their data as well as make steps to protect people's civil liberties and privacy. Police departments may increasingly need personnel with security clearances—including possible high-level clearance in departments that are involved in homeland security and other high-sensitivity issues. They will also require data managers to create and implement an integrated and cohesive plan to maintain the security of data used by the department and its partners.

Finally, as backroom data management and processing takes on a more pivotal role in policing, there will be an increased need for technologically savvy personnel who can manipulate the data in creative and useful ways to get the most out of technology investments. "Backroom" researching and investigating operations will become relatively more central, perhaps lessening the need for on-the-street investigations. In terms of manpower, the trend in using data to model crime rates, demographic changes, and other items of importance may result in an increasing need for data scientists—modelers, econometricians, and operations research analysts—on the staff of police departments. At the same time, if this kind of data searching and analysis could be contracted out to private security agencies, it could free up precious resources to put more personnel in the community as opposed to sifting through data.

All of these changes carry with them the potential to integrate civilians into the police department. The tasks discussed above are not jobs that need be restricted only to sworn police officers—even data analysis for intelligence purposes, which has largely been a task reserved only for "trusted" sworn officials. Although police departments have traditionally felt constrained by the bifurcation of tasks between civilians and sworn officers (Ratcliffe, 2007), the potential for civilians to contribute to the workforce within police departments in meaningful ways will grow as manpower needs evolve away from officers. To cite a mundane example, it probably does not make sense for officers to take fingerprints; better to leave that task to civilians who could be cheaper and, able to specialize, perhaps better as well.

Money is driving departments to increase the share of civilians in their ranks. George Gascón, the former police chief of Mesa, Arizona, for instance, was challenged with the dual realities of officer shortages and the increased cost of officer salaries. His proposed model of policing incorporates the increased employment of non-sworn employees to handle administrative duties formerly handled by sworn officers. This increased use of civilians is not new, and, in Mesa, civilians were already tasked with investigating property crimes, taking minor traffic reports, and gathering forensic evidence at crime scenes. Chandler, Arizona, an East Valley neighbor, has volunteers who write tickets for certain vehicle infractions. The goals of incorporating civilians are manifold: serving customers better, letting police officers concentrate on what they are trained for—crime fighting—and lowering costs, especially by lowering pension costs over the long run. The obvious tension is finding the balance between creating efficiencies and short-changing cities of needed police officers (McDevitt, 2008).

In Mesa, under the direction of Gascón, the program was rolled out in one district in 2009. It has since been expanded across the city, covering a population of 460,000. In its first year of operation in the

Mesa district with civilian investigators, response time for emergency calls dropped 9 percent, as compared with a citywide reduction of 5 percent. However, critics of the program worry about tainted evidence, missed evidence, and the improper storage, handling, or collection of evidence, any of which would lead to a weakening of a criminal case on cross-examination (Coté, 2010).

Gascón's ideas were modeled on Britain's use of "community support officers" dating back to 2001. He took those ideas with him when he became chief in San Francisco. One was using civilian investigators to conduct nonviolent police work, which was modeled on a similar program he had initiated in Mesa in 2009. The San Francisco program is a pilot that will see civilian investigators operating in one or two of the ten district stations beginning in 2011. Responsibilities for the civilian investigators include witness interviews, writing reports, and evidence collection. While there is an economic component—civilian investigators' starting salaries range from $47,000 to $57,000, compared with police officers' base salaries, which range from $88,000 to $110,000—the larger aim is to improve response time to less-violent crimes and to concentrate police officers in the role in which they are singularly trained, getting bad guys off the streets.

Constraints on Changing ConOps

Changing ConOps means changing organizational culture, and that is always a daunting task, as the FBI example below demonstrates. Yet, beyond the organization itself, there are other constraints on change. The most obvious of those are monetary, considerations of budget sharpened by the nation's very slow emergence from economic crisis and the straits afflicting states and cities. That puts a premium on doing more for less, leveraging technology to both improve efficiency and save money—something often said but seldom done. However, many other barriers exist and deserve consideration. The police force at large faces cultural resistance at adopting new policies. In addition, political and legal concerns may preclude many of the options that planners might envision for the future of policing. Effective policing requires innovation in practices. Unfortunately, the protection of public safety does not possess unlimited resources, and the development of new methods of policing, whether through new analytical tools or the possession of latest technologies, ultimately requires investments that are not available to the public police force writ large.

The Challenge of Changing Cultures: The FBI as a Case in Point

As with all organizations, police departments across the country face cultural and institutional barriers to change. Changing missions and goals of an agency are incredibly difficult, and this operational consideration is just as important when considering the implementation of broad changes to the police forces of the United States. The issue is further complicated by the autonomous nature of police jurisdictions— understanding one unit does not mean that a policymaker has full comprehension of the institutional barriers to change. Some key considerations include understanding the answer to the following questions:

- What does it take to change standardized practices?
- Is it even possible to convince the police force to change with the speed that criminal elements often manage?
- How long does it take to change an organizational culture?
- When will training changes really lead to tangible results?

The reshaping of the FBI in the wake of the September 11 attacks is a case in point for both the challenge of changing cultures and the possibilities of doing so, even in police organizations. The September 11 attacks "prompted immediate calls for the establishment of a new domestic intelligence service, separate from the FBI" ("Strategic Policy Issues," 2008, p. 42). Senator Bob Graham (D-Fla.) said, "I think [it is time] to look seriously at an alternative [to the FBI approach], which is to do as . . . many other nations have done, and that is to put their domestic intelligence in a non law enforcement agency" (Frank, 2002). The 9/11 Commission's diagnosis pointed straight at the limitations imposed by the FBI's culture of case-based law enforcement, saying that FBI agents were "trained to build cases, [and] developed information in support of their own cases, not as part of a broader more strategic [intelligence] effort" (National Commission on Terrorist Attacks Upon the United States, 2004). An example is recounted in an article on reshaping the intelligence community regarding

> the case of Zacarias Moussaoui, the so-called "twentieth hijacker," now serving a life sentence for conspiracy to commit murder. When agents from the local FBI field office looked in August 2001 at the flying lessons he had been taking at a Norman, Oklahoma school, they did so in ignorance of the fact that the same field office had been interested in the same flight school two years earlier because a man thought to be Osama bin Laden's pilot had trained there. ("Strategic Policy Issues," 2008, pp. 42–43)

The article then discusses how the FBI responded:

> FBI director Robert S. Mueller, who had been in the post for one week on 11 September 2001, was keenly aware of the pressure to cede domestic intelligence to a new agency. He moved quickly to reorient the bureau toward prevention and intelligence, sending a reorganisation plan to Congress in November 2001. ("Strategic Policy Issues," 2008, p. 43)

Later, neither the 9/11 nor the Weapons of Mass Destruction commission found "the arguments for creating a separate domestic intelligence service . . . persuasive and [opted to give] . . . the FBI . . . time and encouragement to build its own intelligence capacity" ("Strategic Policy Issues," 2008, p. 43). The Bureau's top priority became, in the words of its website, to "protect the United States from terrorist attack" ("Strategic Policy Issues," 2008, p. 43). FBI field offices around the country had been fiefdoms, but Mueller centralized management of the Bureau's counterterrorism program on the argument that there is no such thing as a local terrorism problem.

The FBI's budget more than doubled between 2001 and 2008, from $3.1 billion to $6.4 billion (Treverton, 2008, p. 48). It increased from 34 to 101 the number of JTTFs, which bring together FBI agents, state and local law enforcement officials, and representatives from other federal agencies to investigate terrorism cases, with Mueller promising that no tip would go unpursued. In May 2003, Mueller took a further step by creating a more independent Office of Intelligence, naming an Executive Assistant Director of Intelligence. The point was to upgrade intelligence. Before September 11, the Bureau was divided between agents and "support"—or, as some have put it, "agents and furniture." And the "furniture" included intelligence analysts, along with other support, from clerks to laboratory scientists. Now, Field Intelligence Groups (FIGs) in each field office analyze and disseminate intelligence and serve as a central point of contact both among field offices and between them and headquarters personnel with regard to intelligence issues ("Strategic Policy Issues," 2008, p. 43).

Embracing the recommendation of the Weapons of Mass Destruction commission, the next stage of reorganization, in 2005, put the beefed-up Office of Intelligence back together with Counter-intelligence and Counterterrorism in the National Security Branch (NSB). The intention was to create an intelligence-driven organization, a service within a service, similar to the NSA and NGA—not man-aged day to day by the Director of National Intelligence but looking to that office for budget and broad guidance ("Strategic Policy Issues," 2008, p. 44). Later, the Bureau created "an intelligence career track (one of five) for special agents as part of its general effort to upgrade the status of intelligence within the organisation" ("Strategic Policy Issues," 2008, p. 44).[1]

The transformation was a sea change for an organization in which agents were attracted and rewarded for being on the street with a badge and gun putting bad guys in jail. For intelligence gathering, for exam-ple, it means looking "at threats in the U.S. and determine how to address gaps in our understandings of those threats"—in the words of Philip Mudd, who moved from the CIA to become the first deputy at the NSB. Pursuing cases, ones typically opened in reaction to some incident or tip, might lead to an arrest but might also leave dangerous gaps in the FBI's intelligence about terrorist threats. Instead, agents should work with analysts to "map their domains," assess the potential

---

[1] This process has not been without its challenges. See Office of the Inspector General, Department of Justice, 2007.

threats in a region, and then build an intelligence-gathering strategy to mitigate those threats. Cases would become platforms for collecting intelligence. Joseph Ford, then the FBI's de-facto chief operating officer, described the shift:

> With this new approach, we want agents to ask if the issue that just popped into their in-box [as a conventional case] is more important than filling a critical intelligence gap. It's all about forcing them to make these tough, but important choices about how to spend your time and resources. (Rivkin and Roberto, 2007b, p. 7)

Terrorism is a matter for both intelligence and law enforcement, and the wall that used to separate the two, including within the FBI, has been all but erased. Now, for terrorism purposes, cases are platforms for investigation. Changing the Bureau's approach is a formidable change in organizational culture. Counterterrorism squads in the field regard their work as important but often do not like it, for it is relentless, unbroken by the closure of an arrest or conviction. For instance, one Los Angeles squad, Counterterrorism 6, traced 5,500 leads in its first five years, but only 5 percent have been deemed credible enough to pass to other JTTF squads for longer-term investigations (Schmitt, 2009). So, too, in many field offices the FIGs and their intelligence analysts are becoming valued members of FBI squads, and not just in counterterrorism. By the same accounts, they do continue to be torn, for what their immediate field colleagues need most is operational support, while headquarters is eager to have them develop broader intelligence and threat analyses.

The difficulty of overcoming the barriers to changing ConOps has been seen in various departments across the country. The Newark police director has expressed concern about his department's behavior in implementing the state reporting guidelines. The police of Newark, New Jersey, have not reported the outcome of one in every ten internal affairs complaints to the Attorney General's Office for almost a decade (Megerian and Giambusso, 2010). Without officers willing to complete basic paperwork, data cannot be collected—a serious limitation to the analytical needs of ILP. Similarly, the Baltimore Police Department has run into problems adopting new technologies (Fenton, 2009). Although the city of Baltimore, Maryland, bought about 500 city-controlled cameras, the police force never fully integrated the technology into their policing practices. Baltimore's former mayor and now the governor of Maryland, Martin O'Malley, has been quoted as saying, "One of the challenges we encountered, and I think this is true of police culture worldwide, is that while drug dealers are quick to adopt and use new technology, law enforcement is very slow" (Fenton, 2009).

However, as budget cuts loom, previously slow-to-change departments may be forced to adapt much more quickly. Bob Quick, former Assistant Commissioner for the Specialist Operations at the Metropolitan Police Service (the police force that is responsible for greater London), alluded to large changes that are likely to occur at the Met, including the review of support and back office roles to free officers to spend more time on operational duties ("Will Cuts Force Changes at the Met?" 2010). Although these proposals have surfaced before, it is in the face of the budgeting necessity that the Met may be forced to change. What is clear is that, similar to other instances of organizational change, reform of the police will require the buy-in of the players involved. The Broken Arrow Police Department in Oklahoma discovered that a successful shift toward community and crime prevention–oriented practices was fostered by organizational commitment and high workforce morale ("Broken Arrow Police Department Leadership Team Working with Agencies," 2006). Since effective policing requires high levels of dedication and loyalty, the importance of these two factors rings particularly true.

Budgetary Considerations and Outsourcing

As budgets in cities across the United States continue to shrink, police departments face the reality of curtailed resources. For instance, Atlantic City has seen cuts not only to its police budget but to the firefighting department and other areas of the public sector, such as its public schools, as well ("Budget Crunch Hits Atlantic City Hard," 2010). Although unpalatable, the reality is that, irrespective of the need for change in current policing practices that is stressed throughout this book, lack of funding can leave the needed changes as only theoretical discussions. As is the case for all policy decisions and consider-ations, the bottom line remains: How much will it all cost? Policymak-ers currently face a host of choices in light of the budget shortfalls in police departments; these include raising revenue through higher taxes or facing the layoff of large percentages of the workforce. Yet, at the same time, policing in the United States *must* change. In some areas, more efficient and innovative practices may save money in the long term, though the public must be willing to stomach a large up-front cost. One other option for consideration is the outsourcing of policing practices—an option that is being debated on all scales around the nation and the world.

In the short term, and particularly in the atmosphere of budget-ary crises, states and localities are sharply constrained in how much they can borrow for operations (as distinct from capital projects). As a result, in dealing with declining resources they face two traditional and unpleasant choices: raise taxes or cut services, including cutting the size of the public workforce, with police not exempted. Residents of Oak-land, California, one of the most violent areas of crime in the nation, faced in 2010 either a nearly $21 million rise in parcel taxes to main-tain its current workforce or a 190-officer decrease to its current police force of 776 officers (Johnson, 2010). While the number of police is an input, not an output or outcome, the concern is real that scaled-down resources could have very tangible effects on crime. More than 100 police officers were recently involved in the arrest of 26 alleged mem-bers of a North Oakland gang, and cutting back nearly 20 percent of the entire police force risks negative trade-offs not only in the future but also in current efforts to maintain public safety. This phenome-non has been seen in all areas of the country. The police department in Flint, Michigan, dealt with its inadequate $66-million budget by focusing only on day-to-day crime and foregoing the option of orga-nizing police units into special units as its budget continues to shrink (Longley and Misjak, 2010).

The budget crunch is forcing innovation in cost-saving measures, as some police departments and cities have also started to look to the private sector for help. Proposals related to privatizing security span a very wide range of options. Logically enough, outsourcing tends to start with human resources and, perhaps, recruiting. IT is another natural, though the difficulties of the FBI are a cautionary example. Outsourcing is sometimes accompanied by sharing, as jurisdictions can save money by sharing the capacity of a private firm for human relations or finance, rather than reproducing the capacity themselves. In the past, departments tended to outsource forensic analysis mostly when they faced a temporary need for more manpower. Now, however, the economic downturn has increased interest in more routine outsources, all the more so as secure web technology lets consultants do work from home (Garrison, 2010).

Municipalities and school districts in Oklahoma have started to lease equipment, whether for fire trucks, police cars, or dump trucks (Lackner, 2010). Similarly, the city of Raleigh, North Carolina, has recently signed a contract with Sparta Commercial Services, Inc., which will provide the city with a new fleet of BMW police motorcycles through Sparta's Municipal Lease Program ("Sparta Adds Raleigh, N.C., to Its Municipal Lease Program," 2010). This option allows the government to finance the cost of the equipment without a down payment and also relieves the burdens and pressures of financing the equipment immediately. The alternative to purchasing equipment up front is becoming increasingly attractive, as Sparta also provides police cruisers, tactical vehicles, and surveillance systems.

Leasing equipment is only one option, however. Governments have begun to consider options that include even more involvement from the private sector. The city of New Berlin, Wisconsin, has considered contracting out almost all of its public services, from park operations and maintenance to city planning and permitting and even human resources and administration (Ford-Stewart, 2010). Policing is no exception. The international police community has already seen integration with private security forces. The Metropolitan Police Service in London supplements overall operations by employing private counterparts to do such tasks as stamp passports ("Securing Your Business," 2010). In Ireland, private security companies have begun to rent out custody cells to the police forces, which not only returns police officers to the streets but has been projected to save as much as £400 million a year (Johnson, 2010). In Britain, law enforcement is increasingly outsourcing parking enforcement duties of traffic wardens or civil-enforcement officers, as cities are realizing that the costs of enforcement can be greater than the revenues received in fines ("Far from Victimless; Parking Fines," 2010).

The most extreme option involves the privatization of the entire police force. Simon Hakim from Temple University is one vocal proponent of this option ("Should Police Departments Be Privatized?" 2010). The growing need for security at a time when police budgets have not grown has naturally increased the ratio of private security officers to public officials, which is about 3 to 1 across the nation. The reasoning behind the privatizing option stems from the arguments that monopoly forces inhibit innovation and more competition generally increases the quality of the product, or, in this case, the policing.

Needless to say, however, privatizing runs into strong misgivings among the general public. In Sandy Springs, Georgia, the police force, fire department, and emergency response remain the only public services that not been contracted out (Miller, 2010), and cities in California, including Pomona and Colton, have rejected the option of outsourcing their policing to the San Bernardino County Sheriff's Department in spite of potential annual savings on the scale of more than $8 million (Pinion-Whitt, 2010). They have made these decisions on the grounds that outsourcing results in fewer forces on the ground and thus decreased overall security. In addition, recent private contracting of security forces in Afghanistan point to yet another concern: that outsourcing will entail a loss of control by and accountability to duly elected officials.

Surely, moving public services to the private sector can decrease accountability—something that the American public at large values. That said, there has been over the last century a sea change in perceptions of policing, from *the* quintessential public service to a service provided by both public agencies and private firms and through cooperation between the two (Shearing, 1992). In an ideal world, outsourcing police services to private contractors could help streamline the process and decrease constraints on the budget. In reality, however, outsourcing not only may compromise the goals of an agency but challenge those agencies as well, particularly when the goals of the outsourced company and the agency are misaligned. For such reasons, Afghan President Hamid Karzai has often expressed his concern about private security forces operating in his country ("International Security Companies a Bad Risk," 2010; U.S. National Security and Foreign Affairs Subcommittee of the House Oversight and Government Reform Committee, 2010).

Regardless of the different solutions under consideration, one fact remains: Monetary considerations will continue to play a large role in understanding effective implementation of future, and particularly new, police practices. Each proposal must be viewed through the lens of cost savings and shrinking budgets. On some level, the fact that scholars are even debating the privatization of the police force illustrates the importance of thinking about efficiency and limitations, especially as the private sector becomes more cost competitive. Although police forces may choose to use these developments to their advantage, planners must think carefully about their options. Irrespective of what may be ideal for the future police forces, whether that be new technologies or new demands on forces and training, trade-offs will continue so long as policing in America is limited by police force budgets.

Legal and Political Restrictions

As has been emphasized throughout this book, police attempts to prevent and prosecute a new generation of criminal behavior will require new forms of surveillance, more use of databases, and new methods of information-gathering. They will thus run directly into the American people's sensitivity to what can be seen as intrusions into personal liberties. In one survey a few years ago, over 80 percent of Americans reported that the right to privacy was "essential" (First Amendment Center, 2002, p. 13). Change may only accelerate in the next decade as the information revolution continues to progress forward rapidly and citizens become accustomed to being monitored in a post–September 11 world. Surfing the web leaves indelible tracks, and soon virtually all American cell phones will be geolocated. For better or worse, someone will know where each of us is and has been recently. Privacy has already changed dramatically—only the older generation remembers when telephone calls were private, conducted in closed booths, not done on cell phones on the street for anyone within earshot to hear.

Striking a balance between intrusion and privacy is hard because the intrusions accrue over time and, individually, are usually not dramatic; only episodes like Facebook's change in privacy rules are visible enough to spark open protest. Moreover, many of the intrusions are convenient: It is, for instance, convenient to get advertisements only for products in which we are interested. Yet, the cost is that someone knows our tastes and preferences, from cars to books to clothing.

All police organizations rely on the trust of the communities they serve and have to remember they are interacting in the "human terrain" of their communities, no matter how much of a cure-all a particular technology may seem. That is all the more so because Americans, unlike Europeans, seem more sensitive to what the government knows about them than what private sector credit agencies or advertisers do. (Though not all groups have the same concerns: A colleague reports that his college students are sensitive about privacy. However, when he tells them that they are all over the web, leaving huge tracks, their response is, "You don't understand. We don't care what the government knows about us. It's our parents we worry about.") Those who propose police reform thus will need to take legal and political constraints into consideration.

A current example is the use of surveillance equipment—closed-circuit televisions (CCTVs), facial recognition, and other surveillance tools to monitor physical space. At the forefront of the debate is the potential infringing of people's right to privacy and other civil liberties. In general, people do not seem to mind the presence of CCTVs in their public lives and, in fact, support them as a way to reduce crime (Deisman, Derby, Doyle, Leman-Langlois, Lippert, Lyon, Pridmore, Smith, Walby, and Whitson, 2009). Interestingly, while almost 80 percent of Americans and Canadians believe that these technologies reduce crime, there is little evidence to support this belief. The current consensus is that CCTVs can deter crime in specific locations, such as parking garages, but do little to stop crime in open areas or to deter crime that people fear most—rape, beatings, and the like (Surveillance Studies Centre, 2011).

Yet the backlash was visible when in Milwaukee, Wisconsin, the decision to purchase a network of portable video equipment for monitoring crowds provoked opposition by the ACLU, which fears that officers will violate the privacy of the citizens (S. Williams, 2008). Moreover, as CCTVs become better equipped and collect not just visual images but also infrared or other types of data, they will be able to see through walls and into homes, blurring the line between public and private in a way that people, particularly Americans, are likely to see as an infringement on a fundamental right to privacy.

Similarly, the recent decision by the Virginia Court of Appeals to allow the police to utilize GPS technology to track criminal suspects without a warrant has drawn the attention of the legal community (O'Dell, 2010). In New York City, the use of surveillance helicopters with strong zooming and disguise capabilities has also elicited debate (Hays, 2008). The Lower Manhattan Security Initiative, which employs a web of cameras and roadblocks to track and deter terrorist and criminal activity, draws attention to the increasing trend to collect more information in the ILP age (Buckley, 2007). Civil liberties advocates worry, too, about the ability of the NYPD to track and store facial images of the citizens who are on the streets.

Complaints to the ACLU brought a review of the New Orleans Police Department's use of "proactive patrol" techniques. The complaints discuss random stops and searches and the recording of personal information, all with a lack of probable cause (Trotter, 2010). Also in New Orleans, reporters from the *Times-Picayune*, PBS Frontline, and ProPublica examined the actions of department leaders of the police department as part of a larger look into the police shootings that killed 11 people (only one of whom was looting at the time) during Hurricane Katrina. There was a great deal of confusion surrounding the order that authorized police officers to shoot looters and marked a distinct change in standards requiring deadly force (Shankman, Jennings, McCarthy, Maggi, and Thompson, 2010).

A study done at Columbia University on behalf of the Center for Constitutional Rights found that, in a span of just over six years, New York police officers stopped and questioned tens of thousands of people without legal justification. The Center for Constitutional Rights sued the NYPD for what it claimed showed a pattern of unnecessary stops and racial profiling. Adjusting for crime patterns, the study showed that officers stopped minorities at disproportionate rates, and, in 30 percent of cases, officers either lacked justification for making a stop constitutional or failed to provide sufficient detail on the police form. The NYPD noted that a 2007 RAND study commissioned by the NYPD found no racial profiling by officers (Ridgeway, 2007). The author of the Columbia study, Professor Jeffrey Fagan, challenged the RAND methodology, which used violent crime as a benchmark, a level that accounted for only 10 percent of all criminal cases (Baker and Rivera, 2010).

Profiling will remain controversial. However, it is worth noting that it has two different uses in policing. The first, inductive profiling, is controversial because it "uses statistical probability and behavioral clues from previous offenders to create cookie-cutter profiles and predict the likelihood of a future crime" (Kershaw, 2007). The argument about racial profiling is in that category: If blacks in some jurisdiction were statistically more likely than whites to commit crimes, would it be appropriate to stop them disproportionately, and, even if that were effective, would it be legal and appropriate? Idaho Senator Larry Craig was an example of inductive profiling, when he was caught in a 2007 sting in a men's room at the Minneapolis–St. Paul Airport behaving in ways consistent with soliciting sex (Kershaw, 2007). By contrast, "[d]eductive profiling involves analyzing the evidence—a tire track, DNA, a bloody knife—after the crime occurs in order to create a profile of that offender and use it to catch him" (Kershaw, 2007).

In Britain, in a victory for British civil rights groups, the Home Secretary declared in July 2010 that Section 44 of the 2000 Terrorism Act could not be used against members of the public. The ruling effectively ended the widely used police practice of stopping and searching people more or less at random. EU courts had previously ruled Section 44 illegal. Police must now have "reasonable suspicion" before stopping someone. Officers complained that, in a time of budget cuts, the higher bar would make their job harder, though, of the 256,000 searches conducted by police in 2009, not one terrorist was apprehended (Slack, 2010).

Finally, the ACLU of Northern California released a study in October 2005 detailing the lack of control of police Taser use and the rise of Taser-related deaths in the region. The study examined over 50 police departments in central and northern California and analyzed Taser policies and training materials. Since 1999, 148 people in the United States and Canada have died following the 50,000-volt charge administered by a Taser. Over half of the deaths took place in the year leading up to the study's release. Of note is the fact that the study found that only four of the departments surveyed had created their own training manuals for Taser use. The other departments relied on the manual provided by the Scottsdale, Arizona, manufacturer, Taser International, a manual, not surprisingly, that significantly downplayed safety precautions. The study also showed that only four departments restricted how many times an office could fire the Taser at a suspect (ACLU, 2005).

Despite these episodes, however, the public attitude continues to be ambivalent, displaying no clear consensus on these thorny issues. The Virginia Court of Appeals ruling on the use of GPS technology reinforces an increasingly accepted view that citizens do not have expectations of privacy on public streets. In addition, the installation of more than 500 surveillance cameras by the Chicago Police Department has received widespread public support, something that mirrors national polls (Nethaway, 2007). This is particularly true of areas where the residents do not feel safe. In 2007, crime in North-East Central Durham, North Carolina, was so high that residents were afraid to leave their homes. Unsurprisingly, Operation Bulls Eye, which increased the use of surveillance in this community, was seen as a generally positive decision by the community ("Security Cameras Are Worth a Try," 2007).

Of course, as crime shifts to and is enabled by the cyber realm, opposition may surface again. Antiterrorism and perhaps now anticrime activities that include the surveillance of phone calls, emails, or blog posts may make new decisions to manage these mediums politically untenable. The reaction to President George W. Bush's PATRIOT Act and accusations of eavesdropping by the NSA revealed just how politically and legally sensitive the issue was (Whistleblower Says NSA May Have Listened to Millions of Americans' Calls," 2006). In fact the more recent public outcry to Facebook's lack of transparency in its privacy settings was so strong that it forced the website to change its policies.

Technology, Jurisdiction, and ConOps

If technology enables new ConOps, the obverse is true as well: As policing ConOps change, so will the equipment and technology needs of police forces. The point is straightforward, but the hardware demands are actually quite numerous. This book is filled with different portions of narratives for the future. Each carries its own set of possible equipment needs or possibilities for the future—whether a new electronic recording device, new surveillance equipment, or new databases that make available the appropriate data. And this account does not include the possible advancements in travel and arms equipment in the future.

Moreover, these are not merely considerations for the future, for precincts and forces are now choosing what software to use to store information gleaned from arrests, patrols, and other policing activity. Each one of these requires the acquisition of computers to support these information systems and the new networks that facilitate fast sharing of information. The possibilities are almost endless for new methods to record, share, and transmit information and are really only limited by human potential. However, again the caution is apt: Technology enables, but the human element is key to the future world of policing. Technology supports human decision making; it cannot replace it. There is no substitute for good human links across forces or for the support of the local communities in apprehending crime.

The connections across forces will collide with one other constraint on evolving ConOps—the seams of jurisdiction. Those raise a host of questions as crime extends beyond previously useful boundaries. As cooperation increases not only within states but nationally and even internationally, how does jurisdictional overlap change the landscape of policing in the future? How can legal differences between different precincts, counties, states, and countries be resolved as demands for the sharing of intelligence and criminal information increase? Can formal cooperative mechanisms, like those surveyed in Chapter Three, be made to work better and faster?

CHAPTER SEVEN

Moving Toward the Vision

Too often, visions of the future founder on the sense that everything must change before anything can. While the vision of future policing set out in this book is not only compelling, but also necessary lest the bad guys become the winners, it cannot be constructed everywhere overnight. So, this chapter begins by summarizing the vision and then turns to specific steps departments can take to move toward it. The book concludes with an invitation to the readers to take over, giving us their reactions and comments via answers to selected questions.

Summing Up the Vision

Recall the vignettes of future policing in this book. Both are quite local crimes—a robbery and domestic violence—yet performance in both is improved through technology-enabled changes in ConOps. Most of the enabling technologies will continue to get cheaper and cheaper. IT is the core, and, for example, the cost of capacity on computer hard drives has decreased in the last half century by a staggering 150 million times (from about $15,000 per megabyte to less than $0.0001 per megabyte). Video cameras, too, will get cheaper, not to mention cell phone pictures and videos. Rapid searches of databases—for tips about what the customer service representative would find when she arrived at the crime scene and what had occurred there before and then later matching the prints she imaged and the cell phone photo to identify a suspect—were critical, and those search tools will also improve.

Notice, too, that virtually all the database work was done in police back offices, what the military calls "reachback." Officers on the scene were and will be imperative, but they may be fewer in number, doing less patrolling to deter and surely less report writing and address searching and more responding to apprehend—or even prevent. Highly touted new technologies can be pricey, but, as the hard drive example shows, the basic direction in the cost of the fundamental enablers—IT, cameras, data handling—is down. In principle, that opens the possibility of win-wins for police—more effectiveness cheaper—but only if police agencies make the changes required in ConOps and organization.

Making use of technology requires having people who can understand and assess it—a need demonstrated all too vividly by the FBI's misadventure with VCF. As the FBI example demonstrates, police will need people who can assess technology and formulate needs. Those people will not be cheap, but some, like the young web 2.0 expert recruited by the Chicago Police Department, may be attracted by patriotism and public service. And so much policing seems tailor-made for automating—searching data looking for matches in names, addresses, and crimes but also prints, faces, DNA, and methods. In principle, the savings in people could be enormous. New recruits, both civilians and sworn officers, will be more IT-savvy than their elders.

This vision of the future of policing is not all that visionary, as the book's chapters have made clear. Most of the technologies are with us today, or soon will be. Some dimensions of this future—for instance, jurisdictions that do not match crime—have long been with us and will be with us long into the future—but are not immutable. A third dimension that will frame the future is also here: Criminals and criminal organizations are adaptive. They will continue to look for seams in public safety defenses, and they will become more and more networked, thus able to learn what works more and more quickly. They will adapt even if we do not.

Policing has transformed in the past and so can do it again. That much is clear from the portrayals in Chapter Two of the four overlapping eras. This history shows that there are no sharp delineations between transitions in policing practices from one era to the next or how those practices develop within each era. Transitions seek to build on the good points of what went before. For instance, as policing now shifts toward an intelligence-led form, involvement in the community remains an important focus. Nor is there any "best" organizational form. Policing in the United States has shifted between flatter and more centralized structures. The political era of early America remains the most decentralized model of policing—because of both the lack of technology available at the time and the political connections that granted police their law-enforcing authority. At the other end of the spectrum, the organization of the police force during the reform era was extremely centralized, as top-down decisionmaking replaced the latitude previously given to individual police officers.

More dramatic parts of that vision are also already with us, at least in part. ILP suggests a form of deterrence based less on the presence of police on the beat than on an increased risk for criminals of being caught. It also indicates a changed balance between policing's front office—that customer service representative of the vignette—and its back office, especially analysts and those who manage databases. Outsourcing of some police functions is on the rise, and it suggests a changed balance between sworn officers and civilians. It also hints at new possibilities for partnership. New companies are developing niche capacities for policing: Palantir, for instance, is a company built by former PayPal creators, specializing in "smart searches" of large amounts of data while meeting the privacy and civil liberties standards of federal law; another company, 3VR, aims to become the "Google of surveillance video" by creating "pictures" that are a fully searchable virtual template of a person's facial features.

But imagine if a Google or other technology giant wanted to become policing's valued partner across a wide range of functions and departments. Economies of scale would dwarf those now present when departments share outsourcing for a single function, such as finance. Privacy concerns would also loom large. Could they be managed, along with lines of accountability?

Concrete Steps

The following are concrete steps that police departments and other public safety agencies can take to move toward the vision, along with examples from the other chapters, both suggestive and cautionary.

Educate Personnel and Leaders

Building internal support for change is critical. For instance, police organizations thought preventive patrol was effective until analysis of data revealed very little difference among patrol patterns. Just as officers are taught how to spot an intoxicated driver, they should learn how to use technology: In some cities, all patrol cars are equipped with fingerprint kits, and police are taught how to use the Automated Finger Print Identification System, a computerized system for matching fingerprint specimens. Education will be especially important as human resource needs change. Departments will need more data scientists to deal with large amounts of personal data and more employees with security clearances to deal with sensitive information.

The use and exchange of possible sensitive personal data on suspects, criminals, and civilians will entail a strong commitment to data safety. The increasing interconnectedness of departments brings many benefits but also creates more vulnerabilities for data to become insecure. It also obscures lines of responsibility for data and information. Data management plans will need to be constructed and implemented to ensure that the information that is being transferred across partnership networks is not compromised.

As well, police leaders will have to change culturally to accept integration. Police personnel will have to learn alternative ways of interacting with the public effectively—for instance, the Boston Police Department and its Twitter feed. With increased community involvement will come increased volume of communication and interaction between police personnel and citizens. This means that the majority of police personnel—not just officers working the street beats—will need training in customer service and client interaction in order to effectively engage the community.

Transition to Common Technical Platforms

This should be low-hanging fruit but does not always seem to be. According to one assessment, the gaps across jurisdictions, like those detailed in Los Angeles, now can be overcome, and "connecting the department with every other law enforcement agency operating in or around the jurisdiction should be the goal" (Simeone, 2006). While ILP, in general, requires integration of information from many intelligence-gathering entities, technically that integration does not required a common technical platform. However, it does require at least a common platform for sharing information. Interpol and other cooperative initiatives can facilitate this process, and bilateral working arrangements are on the rise—for instance, allowing officers from other jurisdictions to pursue investigations across those jurisdictions even when the jurisdiction lines are national borders.

In Los Angeles, the LA-SafetyNet initiative aims to connect 34,000 first responders across the county's different police, fire, and public health jurisdictions. Yet, these initial efforts are being constructed before there is any broad agreement on standards for equipment and networks. As a result, there is no guarantee that other jurisdictions that seek to join the networks in the future will be operating, literally, on the same wavelength. Los Angeles County pioneered the process with the TEW group, which began in the mid-1990s. It was explicitly designed to anticipate emerging threats, especially terrorism, and to try to deny networked adversaries the advantage of working in the seams of existing policing organizations. It sought to blend networking with traditional organization by including law enforcement, fire service, and health authorities at all levels of government (Sullivan, 2001, p. 124).

Biometrics, such as blood samples, iris scans, and DNA typing, may come to replace fingerprinting as cheaper, more precise ways of identifying criminals. As well, they may be able to serve as unique identifiers across databases, yielding more accurate cross-database search results. The advent and rapid improvement of database management and biometric technology facilitates information exchange. The FBI is in the process of developing a database of biometrics called Next Generation Identification that will share standards held by Britain, Canada, Australia, and New Zealand and will interface with the NCIC database to further the goal of instant and seamless cross-border information-sharing.

Leverage Winning Technologies

Over time, winning technologies are those used for *collecting, sorting, storing, and recalling information.* Computer terminals in their cars, followed by handheld devices, gave officers on patrol access to information systems, enabling them to check quickly for stolen vehicles or outstanding warrants. PDAs and mobile computing systems are likely to have a major impact, as well as improvements in camera tech and programs designed to interface with them. Supercomputing will be the next step in transforming police investigations—the ability to store, categorize, and retrieve massive amounts of data in a few seconds. The searchable data stored by programs like 3VR's could save hundreds of man-hours, freeing up human resources for tasks that computers cannot do. Not only can cameras hooked up to powerful software detect facial and other identifying features, but they can also be programmed to "learn" normal human behavior in order to detect unusual or suspicious behavior.

Leverage Changing Police, Public, and Private Interactions and Relations

For example, to address its shortcomings in video recording surveillance, the Dallas Police Department Narcotics Unit turned to the private sector. A detective from its Technical Operations Unit worked with a local company to devise a new and improved video system. AT&T partnered with the FBI to allow it access to AT&T's call records after 9/11. When Mississippi Senator John Burton's Chevy Impala was stolen, he called OnStar; OnStar then called the police. When officers had the vehicle in sight, they requested that Stolen Vehicle Slowdown be initiated, and the vehicle was safely slowed to a stop (Crofoot, 2010). Several technology firms and financial companies have regular meetings with police officials in the areas in which they operate in order to keep police abreast of new and emerging trends—for example, in identity fraud. The Boston Police Department has a weblog and a

Twitter feed to alert Bostonians to activities of interest and keep them informed of goings-on in the city.

Draw Maximum Benefit from Federal Leadership and Funding

Here, the spillover from the fight against terror is positive, providing both funding and some leadership. To be sure, terrorism gets a much larger share of resources than its societal damage would warrant, but departments have turned that aid into all-hazards assistance. Terrorism also spurs the trend toward ILP. In addition, it provides incentive for integrated efforts. The story of the public safety wireless network is still unfinished, but the transition from analog to digital television at least freed up space on the spectrum for an integrated public safety network. For all their shortcomings, the fusion centers are another example: "They are intended to complement the JTTFs. If JTTFs work on cases once identified, the fusion centers are meant to assemble *strategic intelligence* at the regional level and pass the appropriate information on to the investigators in the task forces" (Willis, Lester, and Treverton, 2009, p. 354).

Readers Take Over

To be sure, the future is uncertain, and the vision outlined in this volume about the future of policing cannot incorporate all possible trajectories. There are many ways that social, technological, and other developments can alter the nature and functions of policing organizations. As a result, it is imperative to have a wide-reaching and diverse set of discussions about the future factors affecting law enforcement; diversity of opinion is crucial to developing a complete picture of what lies over the horizon.

On that note, we would like to ask you, our informed readers, about your own thoughts relating to the future directions of policing organizations. Please take a few moments to think about the questions below and send your responses to gregt@rand.org. Your feedback and comments are highly valuable to us, as well as important contributions to the debate on future policing. We promise our best effort to respond to your thoughtful responses to these questions with equally thoughtful emailed reactions.

Questions for Consideration

1. What do you see as the functions or roles of police and law enforcement organizations that can be completely outsourced to private organizations, if any?
2. What portion of your officers have (if you are a law enforcement manager) or should have (if you are an observer) assigned smartphones or other PDAs?
3. What are the major social and economic forces that you see as drivers of change in the way police departments will conduct operations in the next 20 years?
4. As this book stresses, technology is a double-edged sword. Besides the advantages, what are the important caveats or dangers of which police departments will need to be aware?
5. What are the ways that police organizations can partner, both horizontally and vertically, in order to integrate policing work?
6. How do you think ConOps will need to evolve so that police departments can respond to new trend developments in a time-effective manner? What will be the necessary paradigm for dealing with new developments?
7. How can police departments foster a culture of proactive, forward-thinking development, so that they can be more responsive and are not left behind by the rapid development through the 21st century?

Bibliography

ACLU—*see* American Civil Liberties Union.

The Advisory Panel to Assess Domestic Response Capabilities for Terrorism Involving Weapons of Mass Destruction (Gilmore Commission), "Los Angeles Area Case Study," in *Toward a National Strategy for Combating Terrorism, Second Annual Report of the Advisory Panel to Assess Domestic Response Capabilities for Terrorism Involving Weapons of Mass Destruction*, Arlington, Va., December 15, 2000.

Ainsworth, Gordon, "An Activity Model to Understand Persistent Surveillance," March 14, 2008.

American Civil Liberties Union, "Unregulated Use of Taser Stun Guns Threatens Lives, ACLU of Northern California Study Finds," October 6, 2005. As of May 30, 2011:
http://www.aclu.org/racial-justice_prisoners-rights_
drug-law-reform_immigrants-rights/unregulated-use-taser-stun-guns-th

American Enterprise Institute for Public Policy Research, *America After 9/11: Public Opinion on the War on Terrorism, the War with Iraq, and America's Place in the World*, March 11, 2005. As of May 30, 2011:
http://www.aei.org/paper/16974

Andenaes, Johannes, *Punishment and Deterrence*, Ann Arbor, Mich.: University of Michigan Press, 1974.

Anderson, R., "Intelligence-Led Policing: A British Perspective," in A. Smith, ed., *Intelligence-Led Policing: International Perspectives on Policing in the 21st Century*, Lawrenceville, N.J.: International Association of Law Enforcement Intelligence Analysts, 1997, pp. 5 8.

Anderson, Teresa, "New Tools to Tackle Crime," *Security Management*, December 22, 2010.

Archibold, Randal C., "Budget Cut for Fence on U.S.-Mexico Border," *New York Times*, March 17, 2010.

Asbury, Herbert, *The Gangs of New York*, New York: Knopf, 1927.

Ast, Eric J., Joshua E. W. Mines, Amrita Mukhopadhyay, Donald E. Brown, and James H. Conklin, "Webcat: Enhancement Through Analysis of Additional Data," Charlottesville, Va.: University of Virginia, 2007.

Baker, Al, and Ray Rivera, "Study Finds Street Stops by N.Y. Police Unjustified," *New York Times*, October 26, 2010.

Barnett, James Aden, Jr., *Statement of James Aden Barnett, Jr., Chief Public Safety and Homeland Security Bureau, Federal Communications Commission, Legislative Hearing on the Public Safety Broadband Network and H.R. 4829, Before the Subcommittee on Communications, Technology and the Internet*, Committee on Energy and Commerce, U.S. House of Representatives, Washington, D.C., June 17, 2010.

Bayer, Michael D., *The Blue Planet: Informal International Police Networks and National Intelligence*, Washington, D.C.: NDIC Press, 2010. As of May 1, 2011: http://www.ndic.edu/press/18507.htm

Bayley, David H., "Comparative Organization of the Police in English-Speaking Countries," *Crime and Justice,* Vol. 15, 1992, pp. 509–545.

Bayley, David H., and Jerome H. Skolnick, *The New Blue Line: Police Innovation in Six American Cities*, New York: The Free Press, 1986.

Blumstein, Alfred, Jacqueline Cohen, and Daniel Nagin, eds., *Deterrence and Incapacitation: Estimating the Effects of Criminal Sanctions on Crime Rates*, Washington, D.C.: National Academy of the Sciences, 1978.

Bradbury, Danny, "Hacker Taunts eBay with Attacks," *The Guardian*, October 25, 2007.

Brady, Hugo, "Europol and the European Criminal Intelligence Model: A Non-State Response to Organised Crime (ARI)," *Fundacion Real Instituto Elcano*, December 1, 2007. As of January 10, 2010: http://www.realinstitutoelcano.org/wps/portal/rielcano_eng/ Content?WCM_GLOBAL_CONTEXT=/elcano/elcano_in/zonas_in/ari126-2007

Braga, Anthony A., and Brenda J. Bond, "Policing Crime and Disorder Hot Spots: A Randomized Controlled Trial," *Criminology,* Vol. 46, No. 3, 2008.

"Broken Arrow Police Department Leadership Team Working with Agencies," *U.S. States News*, June 16, 2006.

Buckley, Cara, "Police Plan Web of Surveillance for Downtown," *The New York Times*, July 9, 2007.

Buddenberg, Doris, "Award Notification: Congratulations Your Identity Has Been Sold," *Freedom From Fear*, 2010.

"Budget Crunch Hits Atlantic City Hard," National Public Radio, 2010.

Bureau of Justice Assistance, *Intelligence-Led Policing: The New Intelligence Architecture*, Washington D.C.: U.S. Department of Justice, 2005.

"California: Reform Over Los Angeles," *Time*, December 5, 1938. As of May 30, 2011:
http://www.time.com/time/magazine/article/0,9171,760373,00.html

Carr, Austin, "7 Ways Real-Life Crime Fighting Mirrors 'Minority Report,'" *Fast Company Online*, July 30, 2010.

Carter, David L., and Jeremy G. Carter, "Intelligence-Led Policing: Conceptual and Functional Considerations for Public Policy," *Criminal Justice Policy Review,* Vol. 20, 2009, p. 310.

Cetron, Marvin J., and Owen Davies, "55 Trends Now Shaping the Future of Policing," i*Proteus Trends Series*, 2008.

Chaiken, Jan M., Peter W. Greenwood, and Joan R. Petersilia, *The Criminal Investigation Process: A Summary Report*, Santa Monica, Calif.: RAND Corporation, P-5628-1, 1976. As of May 1, 2011:
http://www.rand.org/pubs/papers/P5628-1.html

Chaiken, Jan M., M. Lawless, and K. A. Stevenson, *The Impact of Police Activity on Crime: Robberies on the New York City Subway System*, Santa Monica, Calif.: RAND Corporation, R-1424-NYC, 1974. As of May 30, 2011:
http://www.rand.org/pubs/reports/R1424.html

Choo, Kim-Kwang Raymond, Russel G. Smith, and Rob McCusker, *Future Directions in Technology-Enabled Crime: 2007–2009*, Canberra: Australian Institute of Criminology, 2009.

Clark-Flory, Tracy, "Is Virtual Rape a Crime?" *Salon.com*, May 7, 2007.

Clayton, Mark, "Hacker's Extradition for Cyber Heist: Sign US Is Gaining in Cyber Crime Fight," *The Christian Science Monitor*, August 11, 2010.

Cohen, Lawrence E., and Marcus Felson, "Social Change and Crime Rate Trends: A Routine Activity Approach," *American Sociological Review,* Vol. 44, 1979, pp. 588–608.

Conklin, John, *Why Crime Rates Fell*, New York: Allyn and Bacon, 2003.

Cordner, Gary W., "A Problem-Oriented Approach to Community-Oriented Policing," in J. Green and S. Mastrofski, eds., *Community Policing: Rhetoric or Reality*, New York: Praeger, 1988.

Cornelius, Wayne A., "Impacts of Border Enforcement on Unauthorized Mexican Migration to the United States," *Border Battles: Social Science Research Council*, September 26, 2006. As of April 6, 2010:
http://borderbattles.ssrc.org/Cornelius/

Coté, John, "Civilians to Answer Nonviolent Police Calls: Officers Wary of Program Set for Test Run in January," *San Francisco Chronicle*, July 25, 2010.

Crofoot, Patrick, "OnStar Helps Recover Mississippi State Senator Terry Burton's Stolen Vehicle," *Washington Times Online*, May 14, 2010. As of June 21, 2011:
http://www.washingtontimes.com/news/2010/may/14/
onstar-helps-recover-mississip/

Davies, Caroline, "Welcome to Darkmarket—A Global One-Stop Shop for Cybercrime and Banking Fraud," *The Guardian*, January 15, 2010.

Deflem, Mathieu, "Policing International Society: Views from the United States," *Police Forum,* Vol. 7, No. 3, July 1997, pp. 6–8.

———, "Bureaucratization and Social Control: Historical Foundations of International Police Cooperation," *Law & Society Review,* Vol. 34, No. 3, 2000, pp. 739–778.

———, "The Boundaries of International Cooperation: Problems and Prospects of U.S.-Mexican Policing," in Menachem Amir and Stanley Einstein, eds., *Police Corruption: Challenges for Developed Countries—Comparative Issues and Commissions of Inquiry*, Vol. 4.2, Huntsville, Tex.: Office on International Criminal Justice, 2004, pp. 93–122.

———, "Surveillance and Governance: Crime Control and Beyond," *Sociology of Crime, Law and Deviance*, Vol. 10, Bingley, UK: Emerald Publishing/JAI Press, 2008.

———, "Review of *The New International Policing*, by B.K. Greener," *Global Change, Peace and Security*, Vol. 22, No. 1, 2010, pp. 152–153.

Deflem, Mathieu, and Lindsay C. Maybin, "Interpol and the Policing of International Terrorism: Developments and Dynamics Since September 11," in Lynne L. Snowden and Brad Whitsel, eds., *Terrorism: Research, Readings, & Realities*, Upper Saddle River, N.J.: Prentice Hall, 2005, pp. 175–191.

Deisman, Wade, Patrick Derby, Aaron Doyle, Stéphane Leman-Langlois, Randy Lippert, David Lyon, Jason Pridmore, Emily Smith, Kevin Walby, and Jennifer Whitson, *A Report on Camera Surveillance in Canada, Part One*, Queen's University, Kingston, Ontario, Canada: Surveillance Camera Awareness Network (SCAN), January 2009. As of March 11, 2011:
http://www.sscqueens.org/sites/default/files/SCAN_Report_Phase1_Final_Jan_30_2009.pdf

"The Detroit Riots of 1967: Events," undated. As of May 30, 2011:
http://www.67riots.rutgers.edu/d_index.htm

Donohue, John J., III, and Steven D. Levitt, "The Impact of Legalized Abortion on Crime," *The Quarterly Journal of Economics,* Vol. CXVI, No. 2, May 2001.

Dresser, Denise, "Análisis: ¿Adictos Al Fracaso? El Gobierno Mexicano Se Ha Vuelto Adicto a Una Política Antidrogas Fallida" ["Analysis: Addicted to Failure? The Mexican Government Has Become Addicted to a Failed Drug Policy"], *Proceso*, undated. As of May 30, 2011:
http://www.proceso.com.mx/rv/hemeroteca/detalleHemeroteca/150894

Drummond, David, "A New Approach to China," Official Google Blog, January 12, 2010. As of May 30, 2011:
http://googleblog.blogspot.com/2010/01/new-approach-to-china.html

Dukas, Helen, and Banesh Hoffmann, eds., *Albert Einstein, The Human Side: New Glimpses from His Archives*, Princeton, N.J.: Princeton University Press, 1981.

Dussault, Raymond, "Jack Maple: Betting on Intelligence," *Government Technology*, March 31, 1999. As of August 2, 2011:
http://www.govtech.com/magazines/gt/Jack-Maple-Betting-on-Intelligence.html?id=&story_pg=1

Ellingwood, Ken, "Mexican President Wants to Do Away with Local Police," *Los Angeles Times*, October 6, 2010.

Fagan, Jeffrey, and Garth Davies, "Street Stops and Broken Windows: Terry, Race, and Disorder in New York City," *Fordham Urban Law Journal*, Vol. 28, 2000, pp. 457–504.

Fagan, Jeffrey, Franklin E. Zimring, and June Kim, "Declining Homicide in New York City: A Tale of Two Trends," *Journal of Criminal Law and Criminology*, Vol. 88, 1998, pp. 1277–1323.

"Far from Victimless; Parking Fines," *The Economist* (U.S. Edition), August 21, 2010.

FBI—*see* Federal Bureau of Investigation.

Federal Bureau of Investigation, "Crime Statistics," undated[a]. As of May 30, 2011:
http://www.fbi.gov/stats-services/crimestats

———, "Organized Crime," undated[b]. As of May 30, 2011:
http://www.fbi.gov/about-us/investigate/organizedcrime/glossary

———, "Federal Bureau of Investigation National Crime Information Center Home Page," undated[c]. As of May 30, 2011:
http://www.fbi.gov/about-us/cjis/ncic/ncic

———, "FBI—Interpol Leads Fugitive Roundup," July 15, 2010. As of June 28, 2011:
http://www.fbi.gov/news/stories/2010/july/interpol-roundup/interpol-roundup

Fenton, Justin, "Baltimore, Britain and Eyes of the Law," *The Baltimore Sun*, December 31, 2009, p. 1A.

First Amendment Center, *State of the First Amendment 2002*, Nashville, Tenn., and Arlington, Va.: First Amendment Center, March 11, 2002. As of May 11, 2011:
http://www.freedomforum.org/publications/first/sofa/2002/
SOFA-2002_report.pdf

Ford-Stewart, Jane, "This Business of Running a City—New Berlin Considers What Others Can Do for It," *Milwaukee Journal-Sentinel*, October 14, 2010.

Frank, Thomas, "Push Is On to Overhaul FBI," *Newsday*, December 29, 2002.

Friedman, Debra, "Tech Cops: How Technological Advances Are Changing Police Work," *GreenwichTime.com*, September 7, 2010.

Futures Working Group, home page, undated. As of December 16, 2010:
http://futuresworkinggroup.cos.ucf.edu/

Garrison, Dale, "Outsourcing Forensic Analysis," *Evidence Technology Magazine,* Vol. 8, No. 1, January–February 2010.

German, Michael, and Jay Stanley, *What's Wrong with Fusion Centers?* New York: American Civil Liberties Union, December 2007. As of May 30, 2011:
http://www.aclu.org/files/pdfs/privacy/fusioncenter_20071212.pdf

Goldirova, Renata, "EU Agrees Rapid Reaction Anti-Immigration Units," *EUObserver*, April 23, 2007. As of February 1, 2011:
http://euobserver.com/9/23914

Goldstein, Herman, "On Further Developing Problem-Oriented Policing: The Most Critical Need, the Major Impediments, and a Proposal," *Crime Prevention Studies,* Vol. 15, 2003, pp. 13–47.

Gonzalbo, Fernando Escalante, "Homicidios 2008–2009: La Muerte Tiene Permiso" ["Homicides 2008–2009: Death Is Allowed"], *Nexos*, January 3, 2011.

Gordner, Gary, "Community Policing: Principles and Elements," Eastern Kentucky University, 1996.

Greene, Jack R., "Foot Patrol and Community Policing: Past Practices and Future Prospects," *American Journal of Police,* Vol. 6, 1987, pp. 1–16.

Grossman, Michael, "Perception or Fact: Measuring the Effectiveness of the Terrorism Early Warning Group (TEW)," Monterey, Calif.: Naval Postgraduate School, 2005.

Hale, C., R. Heaton, and S. Uglow, "Uniform Styles? Aspects of Police Centralization in England and Wales," *Policing and Society*, Vol. 14, No. 3, 2004, pp. 291–312.

Hale, George Wesley, and William T. Sellers, *Police and Prison Cyclopaedia*, Boston, Mass.: W. L. Richardson Company, 1893.

Hambling, David, "Future Police: Meet the UK's Armed Robot Drones," *Wired*, February 10, 2010.

Harcourt, Bernard E., *Illusion of Order: The False Promise of Broken Windows Policing*, Cambridge, Mass.: Harvard University Press, 2001.

Hays, Tom, "In New York City, the Skies Have Eyes," *The Virginian-Pilot*, May 25, 2008.

Heaton, Paul, *Hidden in Plain Sight: What Cost-of-Crime Research Can Tell Us About Investing in Police*, Santa Monica, Calif.: RAND Corporation, OP-279-ISEC, 2010. As of May 30, 2011:
http://www.rand.org/pubs/occasional_papers/OP279.html

Helm, Mark, "Modern Criminals Go High-Tech," *PC Magazine Online*, July 12, 2001.

Huff, Steve, "Boston Police Have Craigslist Murder Suspect, Philip Markoff, in Custody," *True Crime Report*, April 20, 2009. As of January 27, 2011:
http://www.truecrimereport.com/2009/04/boston_police_have_craigslist.php

IACP—*see* International Association of Chiefs of Police.

Iden, Ronald L., "Bio-Terrorism," Testimony Before the House Committee on Government Reform, Subcommittee on Government Efficiency, Financial Management and Intergovernmental Relations, Washington D.C., March 28, 2002.

International Association of Chiefs of Police, "About IACP," 2011. As of August 3, 2011:
http://www.theiacp.org/About/tabid/57/Default.aspx

"International Security Companies a Bad Risk," *Townsville Bulletin* (Australia), August 9, 2010, p. 13.

Internet Game Exchange, home page, 2011. As of January 20, 2011:
http://www.igxe.com/

Investigation Discovery, "About the *Undercover* Series," Discovery Communications, 2011. As of August 3, 2011:
http://investigation.discovery.com/tv/undercover/episode-guide/episode-guide.html

Jacob, Jacob H., and Michael J. Rich, "The Effects of Police on Crime: A Second Look," *Law and Society Review,* Vol. 15, 1981, pp. 109–122.

Jeffreys-Jones, Rhodri, *The FBI: A History*, New Haven, Conn.: Yale University Press, 2007.

Jeffries, Judson L., *On the Ground: The Black Panther Party in Communities Across America*, Jackson, Miss.: University Press of Mississippi, 2010.

Joanes, Ana, "Does the New York City Policy Department Deserve Credit for the Decline in New York City's Homicide Rates? A Cross-City Comparison of Policing Strategies and Homicide Rates," *Columbia Journal of Law and Social Problems*, Vol. 33, 2000, pp. 265–311.

Johnson, Chip, "Council, Mayor Need to Stop Foot Dragging," *The San Francisco Chronicle*, May 21, 2010.

Karlinsky, Neal, Sharde Miller, and Lee Ferran, "Craigslist Diamond Murder: How to Protect Yourself," ABC News, May 6, 2010. As of December 13, 2010: http://abcnews.go.com/GMA/craigslist-diamond-murder-protect/story?id=10568167&page=1

Karmen, Andrew, *New York Murder Mystery: The True Story Behind the Crime Crash of the 1990s*, New York: New York University Press, 2000.

Keizer, Kees, Siegwart Lindenberg, and Linda Steg, "The Spreading of Disorder," *Science*, Vol. 322, No. 5908, December 12, 2008, pp. 1681–1685.

Kelling, George L., and Mark H. Moore, "The Evolving Strategy of Policing," *Perspectives on Policing*, No. 4, Washington, D.C.: National Institute of Justice, November 1988.

Kelling, George L., Tony Pate, Duane Dieckman, and Charles E. Brown, *The Kansas City Preventive Patrol Experiment: A Summary Report*, Washington, D.C.: Police Foundation, 1974. As of May 30, 2011: http://www.policefoundation.org/pdf/kcppe.pdf

Kelling, George L., and William H. Sousa, Jr., *Do Police Matter? An Analysis of the Impact of New York City's Police Reforms*, New York: Manhattan Institute for Policy Research, Civic Report 22, December 2001. As of June 27, 2011: http://www.manhattan-institute.org/html/cr_22.htm

Kelling, George L., and James Q. Wilson, "Broken Windows," *The Atlantic*, March 1982, pp. 29–38.

Kershaw, Sarah, "Acting Like a Usual Suspect," *New York Times*, October 21, 2007.

Kessler, David A., and Diane Borella, "Taking Back Druid Hills: An Evaluation of a Community Policing Effort in Birmingham, Alabama," *Law & Policy*, Vol. 19, No. 1, January 1997, pp. 95–115.

Kessler, David A., and Sheila Duncan, "The Impact of Community Policing in Four Houston Neighborhoods," *Evaluation Review,* Vol. 20, 1996, pp. 627–669.

Klockars, Carl B., ed., *Thinking About Police: Contemporary Readings*, New York: McGraw-Hill, 1983.

Koper, Christopher S., "Just Enough Police Presence: Reducing Crime and Disorderly Behavior by Optimizing Patrol Time in Crime Hot Spots," *Justice Quarterly,* Vol. 12, No. 4, 1995, pp. 649–672.

Lackner, Kevin, "Equipment Leasing Provides Flexibility," *Tulsa World* (Oklahoma), August 12, 2010, p. E4.

Leonard, Tom, "Maywood: A Model for Us All? The US City Sacked All Its Staff to Stave Off Bankruptcy—and Its Citizens Think Services Are Now Better," *The Daily Telegraph* (London), July 31, 2010, p. 29.

LexisNexis Academic, "Major World Publications Category," undated.

Leyden, John, "Remote Access Tech Nabs Smut-Fan Laptop Theft Suspect," *The Register*, October 2, 2008.

Longley, Kristin, and Laura Misjak, "Fear Factor: Looming Flint Police Layoffs Worry Some; Numbers Suggest Department Already Stretched Too Thin," *Flint Journal* (Michigan), March 14, 2010.

Lynn, William J., III, "Defending a New Domain: The Pentagon's Cyberstrategy," Washington, D.C.: U.S. Department of Defense, 2010. As of May 1, 2011: http://www.defense.gov/home/features/2010/0410_cybersec/lynn-article1.aspx

Maguire, Mike, and Tim John, "Intelligence Led Policing, Managerialism and Community Engagement: Competing Priorities and the Role of the National Intelligence Model in the UK," *Policing and Society: An International Journal of Research and Policy*, Vol. 16, No. 1, 2006, pp. 67–85.

Markle Task Force on National Security in the Information Age, *Creating a Trusted Network for Homeland Security: Second Report of the Markle Foundation Task Force*, New York City: The Markle Foundation, December 1, 2003.

Masse, Todd, Siobhan O'Neil, and John Rollins, *Fusion Centers: Issues and Options for Congress*, Congressional Research Service, July 6, 2007 As of May 30, 2011: http://epic.org/privacy/fusion/crs_fusionrpt.pdf

Mayor of the City of Los Angeles, "$155 Million Grant for Public Safety Broadband Network," Los Angeles, Calif., September 27, 2010.

McDevitt, Katie, "Mesa Looking to Civilians to Aid in Police Work: Volunteers Would Free up Officers for More Important Tasks," *East Valley Tribune*, July 2, 2008.

McGarrell, Edmund F., Steven Chermak, Alexander Weiss, and Jeremy Wilson, "Reducing Firearms Violence Through Directed Police Patrol," *Criminology & Public Policy*, Vol. 1, No. 1, 2001, pp. 119–148.

McGarrell, Edmund F., Joshua D. Freilich, and Steven Chermak, "Intelligence-Led Policing As a Framework for Responding to Terrorism," *Journal of Contemporary Criminal Justice*, Vol. 23, No. 2, May 2007, pp. 142–158.

McGroddy, James C., and Herbert S. Lin, eds., *A Review of the FBI's Trilogy Information Technology Modernization Program*, Washington, D.C.: National Research Council, National Academies Press, 2004.

Megerian, Chris, and David Giambusso, "Police Director Expresses Frustration, Mccarthy Defends Efforts at Reform," *The Star-Ledger* (Newark, New Jersey), September 16, 2010, p. 001.

"Mexico Drug War Murders," undated. As of May 31, 2011:
https://spreadsheets.google.com/ccc?key=
0AonYZs4MzlZbdHU3cVdwbmVLaWpoMkJOcU5BZlFVcUE&hl=en#gid=0

Miller, Chaz, "Circular File: Share the Load—Privatization Offers Local Governments Flexibility and Savings," *Waste360*, August 1, 2010. As of May 23, 2011:
http://wasteage.com/Waste_Legislation/privatization-benefits-201008/

"Monrovia Officials Comment on Proposed Initiative Measure," Targeted News Service, September 29, 2010.

Mueller, Robert S., "Statement of Robert S. Mueller, III, Director, Federal Bureau of Investigation, Hearing Before the United States Senate Committee on Appropriations Subcommittee on Commerce, Justice, State and the Judiciary," Washington, D.C., February 3, 2005.

National Advisory Commission on Criminal Justice Standards and Goals, *A National Strategy to Reduce Crime*, Washington, D.C.: United States Government Printing Office, 1973.

National Commission on Terrorist Attacks Upon the United States, "Law Enforcement, Counterterrorism, and Intelligence Collection in the United States Prior to 9/11: Staff Statement No. 9," Washington, D.C., 2004.

National Counterterrorism Center, *NCTC Report on Terrorism*, Washington D.C., April 30, 2010. As of May 30, 2011:
http://www.nctc.gov/witsbanner/docs/2009_report_on_terrorism.pdf

National Crime Information Center, home page, undated. As of May 31, 2011:
http://www.fbi.gov/about-us/cjis/ncic/ncic

National Criminal Intelligence Service, *The National Intelligence Model*, London: National Criminal Intelligence Service, 2000.

National Drug Intelligence Center, *National Drug Threat Assessment 2010*, Document ID 2010-Q0317-001, Johnstown, Pa., February 2010. As of May 23, 2011:
http://www.justice.gov/ndic/pubs38/38661/index.htm#Contents

Nauert, Heather, "Update: Suspect Charged in Craigslist Nanny Murder," *FOXNews*, October 30, 2007. As of December 13, 2010:
http://www.foxnews.com/story/0,2933,306317,00.html

NCIC—*see* National Crime Information Center.

NCIS—*see* National Criminal Intelligence Service.

Nethaway, Rowland, "No Longer on Candid Camera," *Cox News Service*, August 3, 2007.

Nunn, Samuel, "Police Technology in Cities: Changes and Challenges," *Technology in Society,* Vol. 23, No. 1, 2001, pp. 11–27.

O'Connell, Kelly, "Online Casinos Will Experience Cyber-Extortion During Super Bowl Betting," *Internet Business Law Services*, January 28, 2008. As of January 20, 2011:
http://www.ibls.com/internet_law_news_portal_view.aspx?id=1967&s=latestnews

O'Dell, Larry, "Ruling: Police Can Use GPS to Track Suspect," *The Virginian-Pilot*, September 9, 2010.

Office of the Inspector General, Department of Justice, *Follow-Up Audit of the Federal Bureau of Investigation's Efforts to Hire, Train, and Retain Intelligence Analysts*, Audit Report 07-30, April 2007.

Olson, Eric L., "Reflections on a Trip to the Border, January 26–February 4, 2010," Woodrow Wilson International Center for Scholars, February 22, 2010.

Osborne, Deborah, "Viewpoint: Policing Conceptual Frameworks from the Analyst's Perspective," in Jerry Ratcliffe, *Intelligence-Led Policing*, Portland, Ore.: Willan Publishing, 2008, pp. 82–83.

Pasadena Police Department, "L.A. Impact," City of Pasadena, 2011. As of August 2, 2011:
http://cityofpasadena.net/police/la_impact/

Peters, Gretchen, "A New Attitude: Mexico's Police Put Bite on Corruption," *Christian Science Monitor*, June 6, 2002.

Peterson, Marilyn, "Intelligence-Led Policing: The New Intelligence Architecture," U.S. Department of Justice, September 2005. As of August 2, 2011:
https://www.ncjrs.gov/pdffiles1/bja/210681.pdf

Pinion-Whitt, Melissa, "Cuts Hover over Police," *San Bernardino County Sun*, August 22, 2010.

"Police Chief: Sag Your Pants, Go to Jail," UPI, July 9, 2008. As of May 30, 2011:
http://www.upi.com/Odd_News/2008/07/09/
Police-chief-Sag-your-pants-go-to-jail/UPI-34351215637490/

Police Futurists International, home page, 2002. As of December 16, 2010:
http://www.policefuturists.org/

Poss, Joe, and Henry R. Schlesinger, "Brooklyn Bounce," in Clint Willis, ed., *NYPD, Stories of Survival from the World's Toughest Beat*, New York: Avalon, 2002.

"Privacy and Civil Liberties Are in Palantir's DNA," 5: Palantir Tech, 2009.

"¿Qué Quieren de Nosotros?" ["What Do They Want from Us?"], *El Diario*, September 18, 2010.

Quinones, Sam, "State of War," *Foreign Policy,* March/April 2009.

RAND Database of Worldwide Terrorism Incidents, home page, last modified May 20, 2011. As of May 30, 2011:
http://www.rand.org/nsrd/projects/terrorism-incidents.html

Raphael, J. R., "The Google-NSA Alliance: Questions and Answers," *PC World Online,* February 4, 2010.

Ratcliffe, Jerry, "Intelligence-Led Policing and the Problems of Turning Rhetoric into Practice," *Policing and Society: An International Journal of Research and Policy,* Vol. 12, No. 1, 2002, pp. 53–66.

———, *Integrated Intelligence and Crime Analysis: Enhanced Information Management for Law Enforcement Leaders,* 2nd ed., Washington, D.C.: Police Foundation, 2007.

———, *Intelligence-Led Policing,* Portland, Ore.: Willan Publishing, 2008.

Ratcliffe, Jerry, Elizabeth Groff, Jennifer Wood, Travis Taniguchi, Lallen Johnson, Caitlin McGuire Taylor, Evan Sorg, and Cory Haberman, *The Philadelphia Foot Patrol Experiment: Research Brief,* Philadelphia, Pa.: Temple University, January 17, 2011. As of May 30, 2011:
http://www.temple.edu/cj/FootPatrolProject/documents/PFPE_research_brief.pdf

Reiss, Albert J., Jr., "Police Organization in the Twentieth Century," *Crime and Justice,* Vol. 15, 1992, pp. 51–97.

Ridgeway, Greg, *Analysis of Racial Disparities in the New York Police Department's Stop, Question, and Frisk Practices,* Santa Monica, Calif.: RAND Corporation, TR-534-NYCPF, 2007. As of June 28, 2011:
http://www.rand.org/pubs/technical_reports/TR534.html

Ridgeway, Greg, Terry L. Schell, Brian Gifford, Jessica Saunders, Susan Turner, K. Jack Riley, and Travis L. Dixon, *Police-Community Relations in Cincinnati,* Santa Monica, Calif.: RAND Corporation, MG-853-CC, 2009. As of May 30, 2011:
http://www.rand.org/pubs/monographs/MG853.html

Rivkin, Jan W., and Michael A. Roberto, "Federal Bureau of Investigation (A)," *Harvard Business Review,* April 10, 2007a.

———, "Federal Bureau of Investigation (B)," *Harvard Business Review,* April 10, 2007b.

Rosenfeld, Richard, Robert Fornango, and Andres F. Rengifo, "The Impact of Order-Maintenance Policing on New York City Homicide and Robbery Rates: 1988–2001," *Criminology,* Vol. 45, No. 2, 2007, pp. 355–384.

Rostker, Bernard D., Lawrence M. Hanser, William M. Hix, Carl Jensen, Andrew R. Morral, Greg Ridgeway, and Terry L. Schell, *Evaluation of the New York City Police Department Firearm Training and Firearm-Discharge Review Process*, Santa Monica, Calif.: RAND Corporation, MG-717-NYPD, 2008. As of May 23, 2011: http://www.rand.org/pubs/monographs/MG717.html

Sanchez, Phillip L., *Increasing Information Sharing Among Independent Police Departments,* master's thesis, Monterey, Calif.: Naval Postgraduate School, 2009.

Schafer, Joseph A., ed., *Policing 2020: Exploring the Future of Crime, Communities, and Policing*, Quantico, Va.: Police Futurists International/Federal Bureau of Investigation Futurists Working Group, 2007.

Schell, Terry, Greg Ridgeway, Travis L. Dixon, Susan Turner, and K. Jack Riley, *Police-Community Relations in Cincinnati: Year Three Evaluation Report*, Santa Monica, Calif.: RAND Corporation, TR-535-CC, 2007. As of August 3, 2011: http://www.rand.org/pubs/technical_reports/TR535.html

Schmitt, Eric, "F.B.I. Agents' Role Is Transformed by Terror Fight," *New York Times*, August 19, 2009.

Schnelle, John F., Robert E. Kirchner, Jr., Joe D. Casey, Paul H. Uselton, Jr., and M. Patrick McNees, "Patrol Evaluation Research: A Multiple-Baseline Analysis of Saturation Police Patrolling During Day and Night Hours," *Journal of Applied Behavior Analysis*, Vol. 10, No. 1, Spring 1977, pp. 33–40.

Schumacher, Gord, "Extra-Jurisdictional Policing: A National Dilemma," National Executive Institute Associates, Major Cities Chiefs Association, and Major County Sherriff's Association, February 2003. As of June 28, 2011: http://www.neiassociates.org/extrajurisdictional.htm

"Securing Your Business," *Business & Finance Magazine*, March 25, 2010.

"Security Cameras Are Worth a Try," *The Herald-Sun* (Durham, N.C.), October 25, 2007, p. A4.

Shankman, Sabrina, Tom Jennings, Brendan McCarthy, Laura Maggi, and A. C. Thompson, "After Katrina, New Orleans Cops Were Told They Could Shoot Looters," *ProPublica*, August 24, 2010. As of December 17, 2010: http://www.propublica.org/nola/story/ nopd-order-to-shoot-looters-hurricane-katrina

Shearing, Clifford D., "The Relation Between Public and Private Policing," *Crime and Justice*, Vol. 15, 1992, pp. 399–434.

Sherman, Lawrence W., "Police Crackdowns: Initial and Residual Deterrence," *Crime and Justice,* Vol. 12, 1990, pp. 1–48.

———, *Ideas in American Policing: Evidence-Based Policing,*, Washington D.C.: Police Foundation, July 1998. As of May 23, 2011: http://www.policefoundation.org/pdf/Sherman.pdf

Sherman, Lawrence W., and Dennis Rogan, "Effects of Gun Seizures on Gun Violence: 'Hot Spots' Patrol in Kansas City," *Justice Quarterly*, Vol. 12, 1995a, pp. 673–694.

———, "Deterrent Effects of Police Raids on Crack Houses: A Randomized, Controlled Experiment," *Justice Quarterly,* Vol. 12, 1995b, pp. 755–781.

Sherman, Lawrence, and David Weisburd, "General Deterrent Effects of Police Patrol in Crime 'Hot Spots': A Randomized, Controlled Trial," *Justice Quarterly,* Vol. 12, 1995, pp. 625–648.

"Should Police Departments Be Privatized?" American Public Media, 2010.

Simeone, Matthew J., "The Power of Public-Private Partnerships: P3 Networks in Policing," *The Police Chief,* Vol. 73, No. 5, May 2006.

Skolnick, Jerome H., and David H. Bayley, *The New Blue Line: Police Innovation in Six American Cities*, New York: The Free Press, 1986.

Slack, James, "Civil Liberties Victory over Stop and Search as Police Powers Are Reined In," *The Daily Mail*, July 9, 2010. As of December 16, 2010:
http://www.dailymail.co.uk/news/article-1293119/
Civil-liberties-victory-stop-search-police-powers-reined-in.html

Smith, Bruce, *Police Systems in the United States*, New York: Harper and Brothers, 1940.

Smith, Sonya, "Irvine 'Chair Burglar' Suspect Arrested," *The Orange County Register*, November 4, 2005.

Soat, John, "Beyond Street Smarts," *Information Week*, November 16, 2009.

Solomon, John, *Part 2: The Unregulated Sector*: Consortium for Countering the Financing of Terrorism, World Check Terrorism Brief Paper, undated. As of May 23, 2011:
http://www.c-cft.org/publication/pdf/TrendsinTerrorFinancePart2.pdf

"Sparta Adds Raleigh, N.C., to Its Municipal Lease Program," *Marketwire*, June 15, 2010.

Stewart, Scott, "The Falcon Lake Murder and Mexico's Drug Wars," STRATFOR, October 21, 2010. As of May 21, 2011:
http://www.stratfor.com/weekly/20101020_falcon_lake_murder_and_mexicos_
drug_wars?ip_auth_redirect=1

Stewart, Daniel M., and Robert G. Morris, "A New Era of Policing? An Examination of Texas Police Chiefs; Perceptions of Homeland Security," *Criminal Justice Policy Review,* Vol. 20, No. 3, September 1, 2009, pp. 290–309.

"Strategic Policy Issues," *Strategic Survey*, Vol. 108, Issue 1, 2008, pp. 33–71.

Sullivan, John P., "Gangs, Hooligans, and Anarchists—The Vanguard of Netwar in the Streets," in John Arquilla and David Ronfeldt, eds., *Networks and Netwars: The Future of Terror, Crime, and Militancy*, Santa Monica, Calif.: RAND Corporation, MR-1382-OSD, 2001, pp. 99–126. As of May 23, 2011: http://www.rand.org/pubs/monograph_reports/MR1382.html

Sullivan, John P., and Adam Elkus, "Beyond Active Response: An Operational Concept for Police Counterterrorism Response," *New Criminologist*, May 14, 2010. As of May 1, 2011: http://www.newcriminologist.com/article.asp?nid=2211

Sullivan, John P., and James J. Wirtz, "Global Metropolitan Policing: An Emerging Trend in Intelligence Sharing," *Homeland Security Affairs*, Vol. 5, No. 2, May 2009.

Surveillance Studies Centre, "FAQs About Camera Surveillance," 2011. As of May 31, 2011: http://www.sscqueens.org/projects/scan_faqs

Tilley, Nick, "Problem-Oriented Policing, Intelligence-Led Policing and the National Intelligence Model," London: Jill Dando Institute of Crime Science, University College London, 2003.

Timson, Lia, "Cyber Criminals Change Tactics; Online Security," *Sydney Morning Herald*, 2010.

Tofte, Sarah, *Testing Justice: The Rape Kit Backlog in Los Angeles City and County*, New York: Human Rights Watch, 2009. As of May 10, 2011: http://www.nsvrc.org/publications/reports/ testing-justice-rape-kit-backlog-los-angeles-city-and-county

Treverton, Gregory F., *Rethinking National Intelligence for an Age of Information*, Cambridge, UK: Cambridge University Press, 2001a.

———, "Intelligence Crisis," *Government Executive*, November 1, 2001b. As of September 8, 2011: http://www.govexec.com/features/1101/1101s1.htm

———, *Reorganizing U.S. Domestic Intelligence: Assessing the Options*, Santa Monica, Calif.: RAND Corporation, MG-767-DHS, 2008. As of September 8, 2011: http://www.rand.org/pubs/monographs/MG767.html

———, "International Policy," in Robert J. Lempert, Steven W. Popper, Endy Y. Min, James A. Dewar, Paul C. Light, and Gregory F. Treverton, eds., *Shaping Tomorrow Today: Near-Term Steps Towards Long-Term Goals*, Santa Monica, Calif.: RAND Corporation, CF-267-RPC, 2009, pp. 47–62. As of August 3, 2011: http://www.rand.org/pubs/conf_proceedings/CF267.html

———, *Making Policy in the Shadow of the Future*, Santa Monica, Calif.: RAND Corporation, OP-298-RC, 2010. As of August 3, 2011:
http://www.rand.org/pubs/occasional_papers/OP298.html

Treverton, Gregory F., Carl Matthies, Karla J. Cunningham, Jeremiah Goulka, Greg Ridgeway, and Anny Wong, *Film Piracy, Organized Crime, and Terrorism*, Santa Monica, Calif.: RAND Corporation, MG-742-MPA, 2009. As of May 10, 2011:
http://www.rand.org/pubs/monographs/MG742.html

Trojanowicz, Robert, and Joanne Belknap, *Community Policing: Training Issues*, Lansing, Mich.: National Neighborhood Foot Patrol Center, School of Criminal Justice, Michigan State University, 1986.

Trotter, Darian, "ACLU Asks Tough Questions of the NOPD," *ABC26News*, October 6, 2010. As of May 30, 2011:
http://www.abc26.com/news/local/
wgno-news-aclu-ask-questions-of-nopd,0,2160831.story

United Nations Interregional Crime and Justice Research Institute, *Counterfeiting: A Global Spread, a Global Threat*, Turin, Italy, 2007.

U.S. Department of State, *Country Reports on Terrorism*, undated. As of May 30, 2011:
http://www.state.gov/s/ct/rls/crt

———, *International Narcotics Control Strategy Report*, 2007. As of May 31, 2011:
http://www.state.gov/p/inl/rls/nrcrpt/2007/

———, "The Merida Initiative," June 23, 2009. As of May 31, 2011:
http://www.state.gov/p/inl/rls/fs/122397.htm

U.S. Drug Enforcement Administration, "DEA History Book, 1990–1994," undated. As of May 9, 2011:
http://www.justice.gov/dea/pubs/history/1990-1994.html

U.S. National Security and Foreign Affairs Subcommittee of the House Oversight and Government Reform Committee, *Testimony of Colonel T. X. Hammes*, Panel II of a Hearing, Washington, D.C., June 22, 2010.

Vlahos, James, "Surveillance and Society: New High-Tech Cameras Are Watching You," *Popular Mechanics*, January 2008.

Walker, Samuel, *The Police in America: An Introduction*, Third Edition, New York: McGraw-Hill College, 1999.

Wang, Yang, and Scott D. Mainwaring, "'Human-Currency Interaction': Learning from Virtual Currency Use in China," presented at CHI 2008, Florence, Italy, April 5–10, 2008. As of May 23, 2011:
http://www.ics.uci.edu/~yangwang/papers/CHI08-AuthorCopy.pdf

Weiss, Alexander, and Sally Freels, "The Effects of Aggressive Policing: The Dayton Traffic Enforcement Experiment," *American Journal of Police*, No. 15, 1996, pp. 45–64.

Weisburd, David, and Cynthia Lum, "The Diffusion of Computerized Crime Mapping in Policing: Linking Research and Practice," *Police Practice and Research*, Vol. 6, No. 5, 2005, pp. 419–434.

Wethal, Tabatha, "Decades of Duty After Dark," *Information Week*, October 2009.

"Whistleblower Says NSA May Have Listened to Millions of Americans' Calls," *The Frontrunner*, January 11, 2006.

Whitehouse, J., "Historical Perspectives on the Police Community Service Function," *Journal of Police Science and Administration*, Vol. 1, No. 1, 1973, pp. 87–92.

Wilkinson, Tracy, and Ken Ellingwood, "Mexico Army No Match for Drug Cartels," *Los Angeles Times*, December 30, 2010.

"Will Cuts Force Changes at the Met?" Targeted News Service, October 14, 2010.

Williams, Phil, "Transnational Criminal Networks," in John Arquilla and David Ronfeldt, eds., *Networks and Netwars: The Future of Terror, Crime, and Militancy*, Santa Monica, Calif.: RAND Corporation, MR-1382-OSD, 2001, pp. 61–97. As of May 23, 2011:
http://www.rand.org/pubs/monograph_reports/MR1382.html

Williams, Scott, "Surveillance on a Stick: Fairs, Festivals to Get Cameras— 5-County Milwaukee Area to Share Portable Units," *Milwaukee Journal Sentinel*, August 14, 2008, p. 1.

Willis, Henry H., Genevieve Lester, and Gregory F. Treverton, "Information Sharing for Infrastructure Risk Management: Barriers and Solutions," *Intelligence and National Security*, Vol. 24, No. 3, June 2009, pp. 339–365.

Wilson, James Q., *Thinking About Crime*, New York: Basic Books, 1983.

Wilson, Jeremy M., and Amy G. Cox, *Community Policing and Crime: The Process and Impact of Problem-Solving in Oakland*, Santa Monica, Calif.: RAND Corporation, TR-635-BPA, 2008. As of May 30, 2011:
http://www.rand.org/pubs/technical_reports/TR635.html

Woodrow Wilson International Center for Scholars, "Mexico Institute Re-Launches Security Cooperation Portal," March 10, 2010. As of September 12, 2011:
http://www.wilsoncenter.org/article/
mexico-institute-re-launches-security-cooperation-portal

"World Telecommunication/ICT Indicators Database 2010," last updated December 10, 2010. As of February 1, 2011:
http://www.itu.int/ITU-D/ict/publications/world/world.html

Wyatt, Edward, "9 Years After 9/11, Public Safety Network Unrealized," *New York Times*, September 7, 2010.

Zetter, Kim, "Teen Girl Faced Child Porn Charges for E-Mailing Nude Pictures of Herself to Friends—Update," *Wired*, October 22, 2008.

———, "TJX Hacker Gets 20 Years in Prison," *Wired Online*, March 25, 2010. As of June 28, 2011:
http://www.wired.com/threatlevel/2010/03/tjx-sentencing/